TEACHING ADULTS

A Guide for Transformational Teaching

RICK EDWARDS, COMPILER

LifeWay Press
Nashville, Tennessee

ISBN: 0-6330-0845-1

This book is a resource in the Leadership and Skill Development category
of the Christian Growth Study Plan.

Dewey Decimal Classification Number: 268.434
Subject Heading: RELIGIOUS EDUCATION / TEACHING

Printed in the United States of America

Sunday School Group
LifeWay Christian Resources of the Southern Baptist Convention
127 Ninth Avenue North
Nashville, Tennessee 37234

Unless otherwise indicated, all Scripture quotations are from the Holy Bible,
New International Version, copyright © 1973, 1978, 1984 by International Bible Society.

TABLE OF CONTENTS

Captioned beneath a photograph representing a man closing a business deal was this probing question: "Is his Bible study changing the way he does business?" It's a question every adult or young adult Sunday School leader needs to ask–and answer.

Even with the proliferation of Bible study groups today, a startling level of biblical illiteracy exists among believers. Many believers ignore biblical authority and are only nominally obedient to God. The way they think and live is not significantly different from non-believers.

To effect change we must teach for spiritual transformation. Spiritual transformation is God's work of changing a believer into the likeness of Jesus by creating a new identity in Christ and by empowering a lifelong relationship of love, trust, and obedience to glorify God. Teaching for spiritual transformation is concerned with helping people live to make a difference in the world around them.

In traveling across America the past five years, I have met many people whose lives have been transformed through an encounter with God's Word.

• A business executive who was willing to unload a truckload of pipe so his Sunday School teacher could share the gospel with the truck owner.

• A mother in Boston who voluntarily served in several churches in the New England area because she was so moved by their needs.

• A teacher in Texas who left the comfort of her own growing church to teach the Bible in a struggling inner-city mission.

These people heard a Bible lesson, but they didn't stop there. They continued to interact with God's Truth, allowing it to change their lives.

This book is a resource in the Teaching for Spiritual Transformation Series. The series is designed to help you develop a Sunday School ministry that has a focus on teaching for spiritual transformation. Each book in the series provides specific help for leaders of a specific target group: general leaders, adults, young adults, youth, children, or preschoolers.

Teaching for spiritual transformation will yield thousands of believers who will give their best service to Christ. Then, when we are confronted with questions like the one above, we can reply: "Yes. His Bible study is changing the way he does business, for the Christ he encounters in Scripture is changing his life."

Bill L. Taylor, Director
Sunday School Group

Part 1
Teaching and the Master

WHEN JESUS TAUGHT, PEOPLE LISTENED. When Jesus taught, people understood. When Jesus taught, people repented. When Jesus taught, people saw things differently. When Jesus taught, lives were transformed.

Would you like to teach like Jesus taught?

Following the resurrection, Peter and John were brought before the Sanhedrin for healing in the name of Jesus. Following the inquiry, Luke records that when the Sanhedrin "saw the courage of Peter and John and realized that they were unschooled, ordinary men, they were astonished and they took note that these men had been with Jesus" (Acts 4:13).

What an amazing statement! Surely the dream of every Bible teacher is to be noticed because we have been with Jesus. Do you feel "unschooled" and "ordinary" as a Bible teacher? Maybe you feel like Peter, a fisherman called to preach and teach. Does the idea of teaching the Bible seem a bit overwhelming? Peter and John felt overwhelmed also, but God transformed them and changed them, turning them into leaders and teachers He could use to bring about transformation in the lives of others.

When Jesus called Peter and John, they had no idea of the adventure they were beginning. It was and is a journey . . . a journey that we are invited to join. It's a journey toward becoming a transformed Bible teacher. But that's not all. It's a journey toward becoming a transformational Bible teacher!

Jesus invites us to join Peter and John as we each discover what it means to teach like the Master . . . to teach like Jesus.

Teaching the Jesus Way

1

by Rick
Edwards

*"When Jesus had finished saying these things, the crowds
were amazed at his teaching, because he taught as one who
had authority, and not as their teachers of the law."*
Matthew 7:28-29

Imagine that you are on a journey. The destination is simple: You want to be the best Bible teacher you can be. Perhaps you teach a Bible study group. You may be teaching a group of believers who desire to grow in their faith and understanding of the Bible. Regardless of *where* you teach the Bible, you want to be the best you can be. But how do you get there? How do you move from where you are now, to where you want and need to be?

This book is your guide. Its purpose is to help you become the best Bible teacher you can be. It will challenge you at first, and then becomes a reference book you return to again and again as your Bible teaching skills develop.

Preparing for the Journey

The most rewarding journeys typically begin with preparation. In this instance, the needed preparation has to do with your own spirit and heart. No book, conference, or program can turn a cold, unwilling heart into a solid Bible teacher. This guide can help you make the journey, but you must approach the pilgrimage with an open and receptive heart. Consider the following questions.

Do you see the need for such a journey? Do you believe you can be a better Bible teacher than you are right now? Is there room for growth in your teaching skills? Or, are you already as good as you want and need to be? This is important because it reveals whether you are still teachable. The fact is, none of us has arrived at perfection. You have not achieved your full potential as a Bible teacher. By recognizing the distance between where you are and where

you need to be, you are preparing for the journey.

What kind of Bible teacher do you want to be? What motivates you to lead a group of adults in Bible study? Is it simply that no one else in your church would accept the job? Or, do you teach from a sense that God has called you to serve in this role? What difference do you wish to make in the lives of your learners? Answers to these questions will help shape your destination. If all you really want to be is someone who delivers facts and knowledge about the Bible, then that's your destination. You don't need this book to do that. If, on the other hand, you want God to use you to make a positive difference in the lives of your learners, then you desire to be a transformational Bible teacher. This guide can help.

In the Steps of Jesus

As we stand at the edge of the path that will lead us into our journey, it's nice to know that we're not blazing a new trail. We have a model and an example in Jesus and His own teaching ministry. Jesus set the course for us in the New Testament and demonstrated what being a transformational teacher means.

Much can be said about Jesus' teaching. The Bible reveals much about this important aspect of His redemptive ministry. No serious Bible teacher would argue with the need for Jesus to be our model. Throughout this book we will consider Jesus' teaching ministry and seek to let His life set the course for our own journey. It is appropriate at this stage, however, to draw attention to one broad characteristic of Jesus' teaching.

When Jesus taught, He taught to bring about *spiritual transformation* in the lives of His hearers and learners. Spiritual transformation is God's work of changing a believer into the likeness of Jesus by creating a new identity in Christ and by empowering a lifelong relationship of love, trust, and obedience to glorify God. When Jesus taught, He wanted His presence, message, and life to change people from the inside out. When Jesus taught, He wanted people to become new people as a result of their relationship with Him and then live as new people in their daily lives. This should be our desire, our prayer, and our goal as well.

Jesus never taught merely to make people smarter. Certainly knowledge is essential to all learning and teaching, but Jesus' ministry targeted a much deeper result. He sought to transform people at a very fundamental level by challenging and changing their deepest convictions about life and the world around them. When their perspective on any given issue was changed, they were transformed on the inside. This transformation led to a change in their behavior. Jesus said, "For out of the overflow of the heart the mouth speaks" (Matt. 12:34).

This truth perhaps is best illustrated in the *Sermon on the Mount* in Matthew 5—7. In these chapters Jesus repeatedly pointed to the need to go beyond an external adherence to the law. What was most important was the inner spirit or attitude that drove the actions. By addressing the inner convictions of the heart and not just outward behavior, Jesus was able to declare that He had not "come to abolish the Law or Prophets," but to "fulfill them" (Matt. 5:17).

Jesus then went on to shock the religious and educational establishment by announcing that "unless your righteousness surpasses that of the Pharisees and the teachers of the law, you will certainly not enter the kingdom of heaven" (Matt. 5: 20). From a behavioral perspective, the "Pharisees and teachers of the law" were the perfect students. Jesus understood, however, what we must understand: Teaching for transformation begins with the heart, not behavior. Consider the following admonitions.

You have heard that it was said to the people long ago, "Do not **murder,** and anyone who murders will be subject to judgment." But I tell you that anyone who is **angry** with his brother will be subject to judgment (Matt. 5:21-22, emphasis added).

Murder is a behavior. Anger is an attitude. Jesus went beyond the behavior to address the condition of the heart.

You have heard that it was said, "Do not commit **adultery.**" But I tell you that anyone who looks at a woman **lustfully** has already committed adultery with her in his heart (Matt. 5:27-28, emphasis added).

Adultery is an outward and visible action or behavior. Lust is an inner state of the heart. In God's eyes, the act of adultery is first committed in the heart.

To follow the trail Jesus established in His own life, we must look beyond each learner's outward behavior and concentrate on the heart. We must challenge atti-

tudes, convictions, and presuppositions learners bring to Bible study events. We must create an environment in which truth can take root in learners' minds and bear fruit in their actions. This is teaching for transformation.

The Time Is Right

Some journeys never begin because it never seems to be the right time. Perhaps you've intended for a while to strengthen your teaching skills but just haven't found the time or felt the time was right. Don't be discouraged! It's not too late. In fact, it may be that this is just the journey God has prepared for you to take at this particular time. The following factors would suggest that this is the right time for you to become a transformational teacher.

The accelerated pace of change is causing people to feel disconnected. The people, places, and events that define us as individuals are changing so rapidly that we lose our sense of identity. The 20th Century helped define all of the adults you will be teaching. For better or worse, it birthed us and shaped us. Now the 20th Century is gone. The places we loved as children have changed. The people we cared for have moved. Adults are asking, "Where did I come from?" "How do I understand who I am when everything about my past is different?" Bible teachers have an answer and can affirm the biblical worldview that God created all things with purpose, and He created all people in His image.

The global environment is causing people to question their place in the world. The Internet and rapid telecommunications are making this a smaller world. Many of us watched with amazement as major cities in every time zone welcomed the year 2000. Y2K concerns made us realize how interconnected we are and how interdependent we are on people all over the world. Individuals are asking, "Where do I fit in?" "Am I nothing more than a meaningless web page among millions that no one notices or visits?" Bible teachers must hear the question and affirm the biblical message that although everyone has sinned and rebelled against God, He graciously offers forgiveness, restoration, purpose, and community through His Son Jesus Christ.

The turning millennium is generating significant spiritual interest and personal reflection. The sense that we are living in a truly historic moment will continue for years. People will wonder what it means and whether their lives carry any eternal significance. As people reflect on the meaning of time they will wonder where time is taking them. They want to know, Where am I going? Bible teachers have a unique opportunity now to challenge the notion that time is meaningless with the biblical view that through Christ's salvation, God is present and active now and forever in those who receive Him.

Yes, the time is right for the journey. The world is eager and listening. You can make a difference in the lives of adult learners and in the world around us.

An Overview of the Journey

The journey toward becoming a transformational teacher will cover a variety of landscapes. Inspirational mountain tops and rich, fertile valleys will be explored. It will be helpful to you at the outset if you can see the big picture and have a feel for where you're going.

If you think of this chapter (chapter 1) as a sort of orientation to the journey, then the next chapter is where the journey actually begins.

Chapter 2 will focus on the most important single element in teaching for transformation: you, the teacher. Here you will consider what it means for your life to become "the lesson," and how to strengthen your leadership skills.

SSFNC

Sunday School for a New Century (SSFNC) sidebars in each chapter will highlight relevant features found in SSFNC resources released in the fall of 2000. See the appendix for more information.

Chapter 3 will explore the fascinating and diverse world of adult learners at the turning of a new millennium. What do you need to understand about the adults you will be teaching and leading in Bible study?

Chapter 4 will lead you through a rich study of what it means to teach strategically. Teaching strategically means to teach in such a way that you are guiding your learners toward specific destinations in life over a specific period of time. It enables you to teach with balance and direction.

Chapter 5 will follow a rural highway that winds through the broad principles of teaching for transformation. You will observe some of the elements that are essential to the teacher and group that want to see lives transformed.

Chapter 6 exposes you to what may be some new ideas. Here we will explore the dynamics of teaching in a group and how the group's purpose can shape how you teach. What is the difference between a closed group and an open group?

Chapter 7 will guide you through an understanding of teaching in a Bible study group that specifically desires to reach people for Christ. This purpose will impact how the Bible study is approached and deserves special attention.

Chapters 8, 9, and 10 journey through a practical region dedicated to preparing for the Bible study session, encountering God's Word in a group, and how to continue the lesson beyond the session. Chapters 11 and 12 conclude the journey with a look at ways we can teach with variety and how the ministry environment can impact the learning process.

Chapter 13 takes us along a special path, giving us a look at how to work with people with a variety of special needs. Many of you have discovered your life journey blessed with one or more special adults. Your path is marked with unique challenges, unexpected blessings, and unparalleled joys. For you, we have devoted an entire section of this book. Here you will be introduced to concepts and resources that will make your journey even more enjoyable.

Maintaining A Kingdom Perspective

There's a difference between being a teacher and being a *Bible* teacher. The Bible teacher is under a divine mandate to pass along the truth of God's Word. The Bible teacher is a kingdom teacher. The nature and life of God's kingdom must be the constant context within which the Bible teacher walks.

Just before His ascension, Jesus gave His disciples the Great Commission (Matt. 28:16-20). This defines the kingdom perspective that each Bible teacher should share. It establishes the principle-driven context within which we teach. These verses reveal that there is one Great Commission for the church that functions in five areas with four eventual results. This principle is called the 1-5-4 Kingdom Principle for Church Growth. Simply stated, the 1-5-4 Principle involves:

1 Driving Force for Church Growth: The Great Commission.

5 Essential Church Functions for Church Growth

Evangelism—The good news is spoken by believers and lived out in their lives.

Discipleship—God's process for transforming His children into Christlikeness.

Fellowship—"Familyship," sharing the common life in Christ.

Ministry—Meeting another person's need in the name of Christ.

Worship—Any activity in which believers experience God in a spiritually transforming way.

4 Results

Numerical Growth—Brings new life and hope to a church and reminds us to be about our Father's business.

Spiritual Growth—Growing in our relationships to the point where Christ lives in and through us in a disciplined lifestyle of Christlike love.

Ministries Expansion—Utilizing the Holy Spirit's gifts to believers and opening doors for ministering to people.

Missions Advance—Praying, giving, supporting, and sending learners as the Lord directs.

The Journey of a Lifetime

The brief pilgrimage you will make through this book will reflect a longer pilgrimage of learning that you and the adults you teach will travel through life. Learning never really stops. As a Bible teacher, you may have the opportunity to influence learners over a long period of time. Many Bible teachers have been teaching some of the same adults for decades. This provides the Bible teacher with an amazing opportunity to watch people grow and guide them to spiritual maturity.

Transformational teaching recognizes that a change of heart occurs most profoundly and permanently as learners encounter the truth of God's Word over a period of time. Wise teachers understand the value of time and the need to let the truth settle into learners' hearts and minds over time.

As a teacher, you are, in a very real sense, traveling with your learners in their journey. So, you are not alone on this path. You may be leading the group, but you should be learning and growing yourself. God continues to challenge you, change you, and teach you through your own study, relationships, and life experiences. Your teaching is only part of a larger journey of life. It's the journey of a lifetime!

Rick Edwards is Director of the Adult Sunday School Ministry Department, Sunday School Group, LifeWay Church Resources, and an adult teacher at First Baptist Church, Hendersonville, TN.

2

by Richard E. Dodge

The wilderness around the Sea of Galilee must have presented challenges for ancient people. Although Jerusalem's streets no doubt were familiar to them, people who traveled to distant cities may have hesitated to make trips without help from someone who could guide them.

I suspect many guides could be found. If the guide was experienced and had traveled the paths or trails before, most travelers would have followed without hesitation. Wilderness paths probably were unsafe for lone travelers, too, because thieves waited in shadows or rock crevices to prey on people.

A trained, dependable guide can be much more than someone who points people in the right direction. A skilled guide can save a person's life, pointing seekers toward the safe trails and leading searchers through storms that can catch people by surprise.

Jesus was such a guide. When He called the first disciples to follow Him, Jesus was not merely pointing people in a direction and sending them merrily on their way. Jesus said "Follow me." He knew the way; He *was* the way. Jesus knew how difficult the paths ahead would be and what challenges the disciples would face.

Jesus both guided and set the example for His followers. When Jesus taught, He *became* the lesson. Jesus asked Peter, "Do you love me? . . . Feed my sheep." Before asking this question, Jesus fed the multitude from a basket of food that contained little more than a meal for one. When Jesus told the disciples they must be willing to sacrifice to follow Him, they had no idea that Jesus would sacrifice Himself on a cross so that we all could have a personal relationship with God, our Heavenly Father. The concept of sacrifice became a living example when a hammer drove that first nail into the hand of our Savior. People watched, many knowing that Jesus could come down from the cross if He chose to do so. His example spoke volumes to those who witnessed His crucifixion.

People watch every action leaders take. Leaders must be more than instructors. Leaders must model their teachings. In other words, *the leader is the lesson.*

True leadership reflects at least five essential traits: faith, commitment, vision, character, and a servant heart. These reflect Jesus's nature and what He wants from those who lead others through His church.

A Leader Has Faith

The path Jesus would lead the disciples to follow began with a profession of faith in Him as Lord and Savior. When Jesus called Andrew and Peter to follow Him, Jesus meant first they were to love and follow Him both with their hearts and with their lives. Faith as Jesus defined it is more than mental acceptance of creeds or standards. Faith is a living and life-changing experience that lays a foundation for transformation.

A personal profession of faith is also a platform from which leaders can help others find the path that leads to salvation. A strong personal faith becomes more than just a lifestyle; it becomes a message we feel compelled to tell others. Not everyone will have a Pauline type of salvation experience. Many of us were children when we invited Jesus into our hearts. Yet our lives were changed forever. As we grew, our faith took on new meaning and grew through consistent personal Bible study, prayer, and seeking the face of God.

SSFNC

Ministry articles in leader guides provide suggestions to help leaders be their best.

A Leader Has Commitment

Giving up their careers as fishermen would have been more than changing jobs in a metropolitan area for Simon, Andrew, and the others whose lives were touched by Jesus. Their jobs as fishermen were traditions they had received from their fathers. They were leaving their homes, families, and family businesses for Jesus. He was calling them to make great sacrifices to follow Him. In return, Jesus promised little they could understand at the moment.

Jesus would take those who followed Him along a variety of paths and trails. Some would wind through the hill country; others would take them along the edge of the Sea of Galilee. Jesus would guide them personally for three years, then He would send them off to become guides for others to follow. By sending the disciples out to do as He had done, Jesus began a process of training and equipping guides who can do today as Jesus, Peter, Andrew, James, John, and so many others since then have done. Jesus called people to follow Him first in faith, then as apprentices who one day would lead others as trained guides to lead others. They could have turned back anytime.

Unfortunately the concepts of sacrifice and living example have become clouded if not lost entirely in the 21st century today. The lack of guides may be reflected best in the continued increase in crime and deterioration of national leadership credibility, but is evident also in many more subtle ways. People today search for meaning in life and for leaders whom they can trust. Too often the people who develop a corps of followers—sometimes even in large numbers—become so self-centered or self-confident that they slip off onto uncertain paths or into uncharted waters. Without the right kinds of skills or equipment, these leaders eventually stumble and fall, leaving their followers groping for anchors in life and searching for someone or something else that can guide them back onto safe ground.

People today are searching for leaders who fulfill their leadership commitments. They want leaders who guide them personally along paths that lead to places of safety and security. They may not know that they are searching for Jesus, but the skilled guides people need today know that Jesus is the Way, the Truth, and the Life, and know they are responsible to Christ for guiding lost people to faith in Jesus.

A Leader Has a Vision

Jesus looked out onto the crowds and had compassion on them (Matt. 9:36-38). As He looked into the faces of people who were searching for direction

SSFNC

Leaders can connect with online resources to develop all areas of their leadership skills by logging onto www.lifeway.com/Bibleinsites.

and meaning in life, He not only saw the emptiness and pain of the people, but also the potential of the 12 disciples to meet the needs of the masses. Jesus had a vision of what people could receive—the kingdom of heaven personally—and who could offer them hope and peace—those who accepted the role of leader with Jesus. With the coming later of the Holy Spirit to empower the disciples—and others who would follow Him—Jesus could see the kingdom of heaven realized in the lives of the people.

Jesus spent a great deal of time personally mentoring the disciples both individually and as a group of close followers. He imparted this kingdom vision to them in countless ways. Jesus had a vision and people were willing to follow because He knew where He was going.

People today seek visionary leaders. Leaders must know what needs to be achieved. Leaders must cast a vision of hope and direction. Effective Bible study leaders cannot wander aimlessly in Bible study sessions without seeing the same pain and hopelessness in people today. Leaders must envision themselves as personal extensions of Jesus, carrying the message of hope, peace, and love that each of the Twelve must have felt after Jesus ascended to heaven.

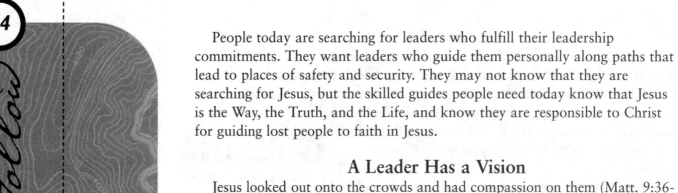

A Leader Has Character

Being good will not get a person into heaven. Jesus clearly states that a salvation experience—being born again—is required for salvation. Character in a biblical sense means more than just integrity and a good nature. A true Christian leader is first a true Christian, a person who is completely sold out to Jesus and believes without question that Jesus alone is the "way, the truth, and the life" (John 14:6).

Character has both a personal and cultural perspective. The cultural aspect of character, however, grows directly out of the personal character of those who make up a given society or culture group. Without a solid, positive character from those who make up a given culture group, the group itself will not have a healthy character.

Character is developed from the earliest days of life. Values and moral standards—the core of character—are learned and experienced from those who

nurture and shape our lives from birth. The family represents the center of character development. Adult Bible study then becomes an arena for helping adults learn both what Christian character is and then how to create a home in which Christian character and values are clearly established and taught.

Christ-centered families will grow Christ-centered children, youth, and adults. Adults who seek to build homes and families based on values and morals headed in a "true north" direction—toward Christlikeness—require leaders who themselves know how to move in that direction.

Character is not something we inherit; we learn it. Just as the indicator on a compass can be changed when the compass is placed near something that has magnetic qualities, so also can lives be pulled away from true north by the pull of compromised social standards. The world creates a false sense of acceptable standards, many of which are not consistent with biblical teaching. We cannot escape the pull of the world. Thus we must stop and reflect on the direction we are following—even make course corrections—to make sure we are following the true north heading toward Christlikeness both for our families and for those we lead. Otherwise we might be leading those who follow our teaching down the wrong paths by the lives we lead more than by the words we teach.

Can character be changed? Yes, just as a heart can be changed, so character can be changed. But we cannot make that change alone. Character grows out of the heart and inner values, and these cannot be changed permanently without the power of the Holy Spirit. Prayer, Bible study, and personal mentoring from brothers and sisters in Christ can be powerful tools in the hands of the Holy Spirit to change the heart of even the coldest sinner. But without heavenly support, most attempts to make character change will be temporary and artificial.

A Leader Has a Servant Heart

Jesus set a high standard for leadership: the cross. The One who became the greatest leader demonstrated His leadership through self-sacrifice. Jesus said that the greatest must become the most humble servant to be truly great (Matt. 18:4; 23:11).

A servant leader is a leader whose primary focus is fulfilling the wishes of the Master. Jesus gave a number of important commands: Seek first the kingdom of God; love God with all of our being; make disciples and lead others to Christ. Each of these commands requires something extra from each of us. We cannot achieve these and so many more commands without loving and serving the people Jesus would love and serve. The model Jesus taught often was one of going wherever He needed to go to get the job done. Jesus went to the home of a tax collector; to the well where He knew a woman scorned by the community would be coming; and through Samaria, a land despised by those who claimed to be closest to God.

Jesus also said that those who made sacrifices for His kingdom would be blessed because of their sacrifices. Christian leaders who make selfless sacrifices of time, energy, and resources may feel at times that no one cares,

Teachers People Follow

that people really don't notice the sacrifices they are willing to make. Rest assured: God cares, and He's the one who will bless our efforts.

The Price of Leadership

The price of leadership is high. Leaders today cannot merely fill positions in church structures and feel they are making a big contribution. If Jesus could look over the multitudes 2000 years ago and see them wandering aimlessly as sheep without a shepherd, how much more today must He weep as He looks over multitudes who search for a guide to lead them to places of peace and security? Today's leaders must become transformed both as Christians and as leaders. How can leaders today become more Christlike leaders?

SSFNC

Leader Guides in all curriculum series provide tips for weekly Sunday School leadership team meetings.

Leaders must focus on relationships. People feel more separated and alienated today than anytime in history. The more technology helps us achieve independence, the more technology separates us from personal contact with other people. We hunger for relationships, often going weeks or more without talking with people who live nearby in our neighborhoods. Jesus knew the hearts of His closest followers. We too must know our followers—our learners—to be able to guide them through life today.

Leaders must value each person unconditionally. There were no second-class people to Jesus. Jesus loved people unconditionally, regardless of their background. Leaders must see each learner as a person worthy of investing his or her time in personally.

Leaders must grow. Every person who becomes a leader also must become a dedicated student of leadership and skill development. Most people face continuous education requirements in their secular jobs, so why do so many Sunday School leaders resist "continuing education" in their Sunday School leadership areas? Transformed teachers are those who seek to improve in every area of their lives, and skill development is one very important area.

Leaders must produce leaders. The mark of a good teacher is not how large a class the teacher can amass, but how many people leave to serve in other Bible study groups or areas of the Bible teaching and church ministries. Effective leaders mentor others to become leaders. Mentoring is a time-consuming and risky process because we cannot mentor someone else until we put ourselves at risk. We first must identify our strengths and weaknesses so we can grow in areas where we are weak. We then must open our inner natures to others. They can see all the imperfections that often go unseen in a classroom session.

Leaders must be team players. True leaders know that the classes they teach are part of a greater ministry, that of the Sunday School as a whole and the church itself, as well as the kingdom of God. Therefore real leaders work to support and encourage other leaders, and offer help whenever needed. At the same time, leaders see their work in their classes as a team effort, one that includes all members. Every person who knows Jesus personally has been given at least one spiritual gift that God intends to be used in His church. Teachers and other leaders must learn to share the load with others in the class and allow others to express their gifts as a fit expression of worship.

Leaders must hold one another accountable. The Bible speaks clearly about accountability. More will be required of those who teach than of others (James 3:1). But all leaders will be held accountable for what they do and for the influence they have on others. Leaders can create informal—or formal, for that matter—accountability groups to encourage one another and to help one another grow. Groups can be formed with a mixture of strengths and backgrounds so that everyone in the group learns from and grows with others in the group.

Leaders must take risks. Jesus promised that all power was given to Him by the Father (Matt. 28:18). After He commanded the disciples to go out and change the world, Jesus promised that He would be with them till the end of the age. His promise included the power of the Holy Spirit. That power is still promised to those who take a risk to follow Jesus. Whether venturing into unsafe neighborhoods to tell lost people the gospel, turning the reigns of leading our "own" classes over to apprentices, or opening the doors of our lives to let others see our imperfections, we must be willing to take risks for Jesus.

Wilderness areas are not the only places where people can wander off straight, safe paths. The trails, streets, and highways of life can be confusing when maps are not clearly marked. The paths to righteousness are hidden often by false belief structures and people who claim to have secret paths to greatness. Only one Guide can truly lead to God. Jesus said "I am the way, the truth, and the life." Today's leaders must be guides who take people to the One who transforms life to the standards set by God in His Word.

Richard E. Dodge is Adult Ministry Consultant, Sunday School Group, LifeWay Church Resources, and is Sunday School director, Una Baptist Church, Nashville, TN.

The People We Teach

3

by Daryl
Eldridge

Writers through the ages have used the metaphor of the journey to describe the seasons and challenges of life. In many respects, the journey through adulthood is like a backpacking trip. Trails through God's creation hold the promise of spectacular sunsets, breathtaking waterfalls, and marvelous sights and sounds of nature. At each turn new vistas and panoramic views can be experienced.

Backpacking trips also include their share of difficulties. Backpackers must ford creeks and rivers, climb mountains, and overcome other obstacles. Dehydration, injuries, and even death can be just around a bend or across a hill.

Each of us will face many similar experiences along the trail. Yet each person's trip is affected by past experiences, abilities, fears, and the provisions carried along the way. Some bring too much baggage; others bring too little gear. Some have physical handicaps or injuries that provide additional challenges along the trip. Because of their outlook on life, some sojourners appreciate the beauty of the trail and the experience more than others. Some are more courageous; some gain more from the experience. Listening to backpackers who have hiked the same trails is amazing. They may have been on the same trail at different times of the year and had different kinds of weather and conditions, but there is a sense of camaraderie between fellow sojourners.

In this chapter the journey will help us see the travels through the paths and trails of adulthood. Keep in mind some key principles as you examine the journey of adulthood. First, all adults of any generation experience similar challenges through life. For example, most adults will face the challenge of finding a vocation, finding a mate or contentment in being single, and adjusting to physiological changes. Adults enjoy being with others who are facing similar challenges and have similar experiences. Climbing these hills and following the predictable paths of life can be exciting.

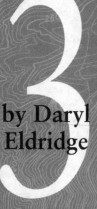

At the same time, each generation of adults is influenced by the events they witnessed and the values that existed during their formative years. To minister effectively to and with adults, leaders must understand the values and experiential base of each generation. There are several perspectives on how generations have been identified. No single perspective on generations has been accepted as the definitive picture of adult generations. Louis Hanks, in *Vision, Variety, and Vitality: Teaching Today's Adult Generations,* identified four specific generations of adults. These included the PowerBuilder Generation (birth years of 1901-1925), PeaceMaker Generation (1926-1944), PathFinder Generation (1945-1963), and PaceSetter Generation (1964-1981). Thom Rainer, in *The Bridger Generation,* identifies three generations covering much the same time frame: Builders (birth years of about 1910-1946), Boomers (birth years about 1946-1964), and Busters (birth years about 1965-1976).

Each generation approaches life differently than do their parents or grandparents. Each generation has it's own identity, much of which has been defined by its music, movies, literature, and events. While adults in all generations may have witnessed the same events, such as the landing on the moon, they will interpret those events and their significance differently.

Adult also brings unique abilities and challenges to the tasks of adulthood. A person raised in a rural setting has a different perspective on life than someone who grew up in New York City. Those raised in two-parent homes have a different outlook on some things than those who grew up in single-parent homes. All of us carry baggage that affects the journey. For this reason, each adult must be understood and known outside of his or her generational "box." An individual's experiences and needs may be very different from others in the same church or community.

As on a backpacking trip, the journey of life

3

The People We Teach

3

SSFNC

Ministry Resources articles are provided each quarter in all leader guides. Articles provide foundational tips for building effective Adult Sunday School work.

is full of storms and difficulties. When hiking, no one can predict when a storm will move in. Storms of life produce stress to those on the trail of life. Moving to a new town, getting married, losing a loved one, getting fired, getting a divorce, or enduring an illness are some events that produce higher levels of stress. Several of these events occurring at the same time compound the stress and its effects. These life events may occur at any time in the life of an adult. Such experiences also are not limited to any generation or stage in life. As you walk through the journey of adulthood in this chapter, consider how the experiences and markers of life provide opportunities for Christians to witness and minister.

Entering Adulthood

Our journey begins with adults ages 18-29. The challenges facing young adults include acquiring skills for a job, getting started in a career, selecting a mate or adjusting to single status, starting a family, rearing children or relating to the children of others, and finding a group of friends with whom to associate. These tasks require a great deal of psychological, emotional, and spiritual energy.

Young adults begin to pull away from their parents and become more independent. This process begins somewhere around age 18 as individuals go back and forth between family and a new home base such as military service, college life, or living in an apartment. Leaving adolescence and entering adulthood involves increasing the psychological distance between self and family and reducing dependence on parental support.

Along with the exhilaration of independence comes the fear of making mistakes. Young adults want to please their parents, but at the same time want to establish their own identities and independent lives.

One developmental challenge young adults face is developing intimate relationships, which require sacrifice and selfless giving. Young adults will either develop healthy, meaningful relationships or will feel isolated from society. Young adults today understand this challenge like no preceding generation. Many are the product of divorce and single-parent homes. Nearly 50 percent of young adults grew up in broken homes. They are the recipients of broken promises and guilt-motivated overindulgence. As a result, many young adults seem to be emotionally callused. They are cynical, suspicious, and disrespectful of authority. This generation understands the pain of broken relationships.[1] Consequently, they are often committed to strengthening families and preventing divorce.

Today's young adults have felt isolated in other ways, too. The term "latch key children" came into existence with today's GenXers. Left alone at home for hours by working parents, these young adults grew up in the company of babysitters such as television, video games, and computers. For many, this child-hood isolation motivates them to seek intimacy as adults.

The value that results from the conflict between intimacy and isolation is love. Friends and relationships are vitally important to this age group. In a word, they want to "belong." They want to be accepted as adults, to be respected and val-ued for their talents, abilities, and enthusiasm.

In the past, the church has said: Behave, believe, and then belong. To belong, you first must behave like us. If you behave and believe like us, then—and only then—you can belong to our church. To reach this generation, we must reverse that message by saying, You belong in our church regardless of who you are or where you come from. Once young adults feel they belong, they can begin to believe. Once they believe, God can change their behavior.

Young adults seek mentors. They need adults beyond their parents who can serve as guides in the beginning of their journey into adulthood. These non-authority figures are generally about 20 years older and can assist younger people in becoming successful adults. Mentors may be Bible study teachers, bosses, professors, or older colleagues.

The 20s are a decade of confidence. Young adults believe they can do any-thing. They are unaware of the many pitfalls that would make them more cautious. They are resolved to be professionally competent. While the Xers have little confidence in institutions, government, and the future of society in general, they have a powerful confidence in their personal futures.

Young adults reject the boomer generation's approach to success.[2] To them, a job is not an end in itself, but a means of achieving self-worth and serving the community. They are not driven by the accumulation of possessions. They are willing to give long, hard hours to their careers, and want their work to be mean-ingful, enjoyable, and make a significant difference in the lives of others. This is a noble generation that wants a more healthy balance between work and family.

Young adulthood has been identified as the least-religious period of life. Many drop out of church during these years. The new tasks of adulthood often pull them away from time spent in church. Out on their own, they are away from parents, who often insisted they attend church. It's also a time of spiritual questioning. Young adults ask: Is this my faith, or my parents' faith? Do I believe what I believe because I believe it, or do I believe this because it's what my parents believe? In testing these beliefs and developing a worldview, young adults may be drawn to fads and cults. Young adults are more likely to be interested in religion if their friends are involved in religious organizations.

Raised in a post-modern world, young adults have been led to believe that truth is subjective and relative. Their's is a tolerant generation, allowing any ideology. A young adult might say, "That's not what I believe, but if it works for you, that's great." They are not impressed with degrees and titles or with what Luther or Calvin believed. They want to know what the Bible says about a subject. They also want to know whether following the Bible makes any difference in life. Young adults are interested in your story, but they also are interested in how their stories connect and fit in with God's story of redeeming love.

3

Young adults are changing from an adolescent view of God as a God of fear to an understanding of a God of love. Listen to their prayers and how they describe their relationship and understanding of God. More than any other, young adults describe God as a friend.

Age 30: Transition

The trip from the 20s to 30s can be turbulent. Men and women alike speak of feeling trapped and restricted. The personal and career choices made in the 20s are impacting or limiting future decisions. Dissatisfaction leads to a serious evaluation of life goals.

This is an especially difficult time for women. Many who postponed child-bearing are hearing the tick of the biological clock. Some choose to invest their energies in other areas. Young women who are pressed by the care of young children may ask, "Is this all there is?" Like backpackers lost on a path that seems to go nowhere, they may feel trapped and lost.

This period may result in young adults adjusting lofty visions and dreams of the 20s to more realistic, attainable goals. A person going through this transition has the feeling that there must be something more.

SSFNC

Leader and learner guides are provided in two general approaches. 1) Narrowly-graded materials for groups that closely identify with generational and lifestyle groups (18-24, 25-39, 40-59, and 60-up) and 2) Non-graded resources for groups with wider age ranges.

The 30s: Getting Settled

The 30s are characterized by settling down, a time in the journey to set up camp and establish a personal home base. Young adults begin to concentrate on children and the quality of family life. They begin putting down roots by buying homes and becoming more earnest about climbing career ladders. Social life outside the family is typically reduced as energies are increasingly focused on raising children.

Couples who concentrate their energies on a career easily can ignore family needs. Young adults may say, I didn't get married for this. Couples are susceptible to divorce, extramarital affairs, and other crises of personal life.

However, not all couples respond negatively to the challenges. Couples who attend church irregularly often begin to return to church. They recognize the need to provide a moral influence for their children and the need to seek help in teaching the fundamentals of faith. Young adults may revive religious practices observed during their upbringing or modify them to fit their lives. Adults in their 30s begin to take an active part in church life. There is a new seriousness about the inner life.

Henry Simmons, in an article in *Religious Education,* suggests a new and distinctive faith becomes possible and necessary at about age 30. He suggests there are three conditions, without which this mature faith cannot occur: affective autonomy, social responsibility, and community sponsorship.[3] Simmons feels that psychologically and cognitively, a person typically has not arrived at these conditions before age 30. It is interesting to note that Jesus began His ministry around that same age.

Young Adult Attitudes Toward Organized Religion

Many young adults today are either somewhat alienated or completely turned off toward organized religion. Some of this alienation is typical of the development of young adults. Some, however, comes from the influence of the prevailing secular worldview. In an age of new morality and tolerance, the church is viewed as intolerant, out of date, and boring.

Don't confuse this generation's criticism of the church with a lack of spirituality and commitment to God. This generation is referred to by some as the "X-tremes." Young adults will jump out of airplanes on snowboards or sleep in tents among snakes to share the gospel with an unreached people group. Many are highly committed to Christ. There is much the church can gain from their enthusiasm. Young adults' zeal for Christ and their desire to make a difference in this world can revive a sometimes complacent congregation.

Implications for Ministry with Young Adults

Those involved in the process of Christian education must recognize the relationship between faith development and other aspects of human development. Ministry with young adults must be viewed holistically if we are to help them progress in all aspects of their journey.

1. Young adults in the process of pulling up roots must receive help to develop their own belief system and a biblical worldview. Their religious beliefs are moving from external (what their parents believe) to internal (what they believe). At this stage, young adults need freedom to question, stretch, and explore without being rejected or put down.

2. A ministry to younger adults should provide Bible studies based on personal and experiential theology. Young adults want to know what God is doing in the lives of others. Today, nearly 90 percent of the population believes in a supreme being. In the first decade of the 21st century, they ask, Is God present? Young adults seek ways the Bible speaks to their everyday needs. GenXers are drawn to issue-oriented Bible studies that include time for prayer and sharing.

3. The church must realize the distance that exists between the Christian church and alienated young adults. Leaders must strive to create an environment within the church that says young adults are welcome, they belong, and are appreciated for the gifts they bring to the body of Christ.

4. Any ministry to young adults must include young adults in the planning process. Young adults desire to participate in and partially control their own processes. A young adult ministry should be a ministry *with*, not *to*, young adults.

SSFNC

Teaching plans in narrowly graded leader guides address both lifestyle and generational issues appropriate to the target audience.

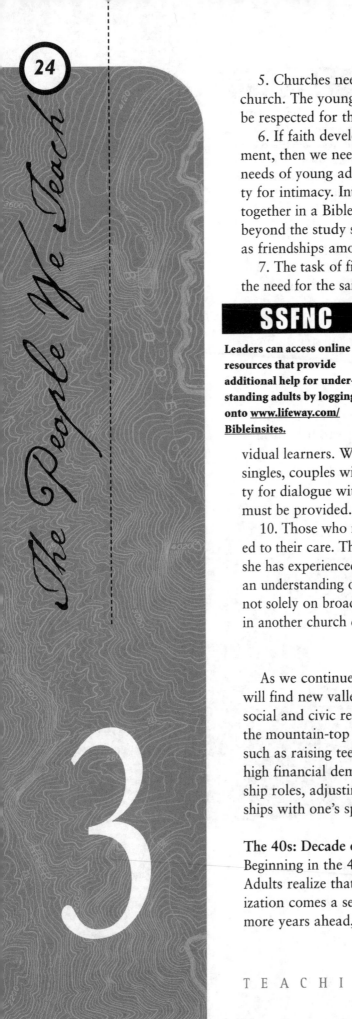
5. Churches need to involve young adults in the total life and work of the church. The young adult years are the most creative years of life. They need to be respected for their value and made to feel they are worthy of trust.

6. If faith development is related to other dimensions of human development, then we need to develop a ministry that will meet the psychosocial needs of young adults. One task of young adulthood is developing the capacity for intimacy. Intimacy cannot be developed simply by spending an hour together in a Bible study session. A young adult ministry should include events beyond the study session that would develop *koinonia*—fellowship—as well as friendships among young adults.

7. The task of finding a mentor (adviser-teacher) in their occupations suggests the need for the same in their spiritual lives. Young adults respond well to small-group Bible studies that expect accountability from participants.

SSFNC

Leaders can access online resources that provide additional help for understanding adults by logging onto www.lifeway.com/ Bibleinsites.

8. The introspection of the 30s and the focus on examining the quality of the family point to the need for Bible studies, conferences, and other discipleship formats on family life and relationships.

9. A ministry with young adults should involve a variety of group interactions based on the needs of individual learners. While ministry organization may reflect various groupings—singles, couples with children, couples without children—plenty of opportunity for dialogue with all of their peers and with the entire adult community must be provided.

10. Those who minister to young adults must get to know each adult entrusted to their care. They should learn where each adult has traveled and what he or she has experienced in life. Ministry opportunities should be designed based on an understanding of the special needs and experiences of the adults in the group, not solely on broad generational stereotypes. Just because a ministry idea worked in another church does not mean it is right for this church or group.

Middle Adulthood

As we continue the journey through life, adults entering middle adulthood will find new valleys and vistas. Peak earning power, leadership opportunities, social and civic recognition, and celebration of family milestones are a few of the mountain-top experiences of this age group. Along the trail are challenges such as raising teenagers, maintaining a standard of living during a period of high financial demand, assisting aging parents, assuming demanding leadership roles, adjusting to physiological changes, and deepening one's relationships with one's spouse and family members.

The 40s: Decade of Urgency

Beginning in the 40s a major redirection from outer to inner concerns occurs. Adults realize that the journey has reached the halfway mark. With this realization comes a sense of urgency. While individuals may have another 30 or more years ahead, middle adults realize the clock is running out.

Signs of aging seem to appear daily. Hair loss, weight gain, lower energy levels, bifocals, longer recovery time from minor injuries, and reduced strength and speed are persistent reminders that aging—and death—while not necessarily imminent, are inevitable. Recognizing these physiological changes influences spiritual development as middle adults begin to recognize and accept death as part of life.

Middle age is like going through adolescence because issues of self-esteem and self-worth reappear. A new search for meaning and significance can be positively directed to teaching and guiding the next generation. The mid-years of life can motivate adults to refocus creative energies in making a difference in the world. The search for meaning and significance also can result in a midlife crisis, particularly among men. Frank Sinatra's crooning of "I've Got to Be Me" would make an excellent theme song for the midlife crazies. In an attempt to recapture their youth, some men leave their wives for younger women, buy sporty cars, join health clubs, or wear jewelry. Depression and alcoholism are also enemies of this emotionally volatile time. Many middle adults find out too late that their self-indulgent behavior only ends in emptiness and impoverishment of the soul.

The 40s call for radical reassessment of life. It becomes important to ask such questions as: What have I done with my life? What do I want others to say about me when I die? What is really important for me and my family? What difference am I making in the world? What is the purpose and meaning of life? This reassessment can be the creative motivation for determining how middle adults will live the rest of their lives. It is an opportunity for middle adults to affirm, adjust, and shape their journey.

The 50s: Self-Acceptance
At the turn of this century, the first boomers began entering their 50s. Like the adult sojourners before them, the sense of urgency that characterized the 40s is gone. At last the trail smooths out and stability sets in. The peaks and valleys of high expectations and bitter disappointments level out. There is now more time to reflect on the quality of life. The achievement of the 50s is a sense of self-esteem due to a realistic evaluation of a half-century of living.

The major challenges facing those in this decade are launching their children and adapting to an empty nest. Married couples that previously focused solely on the children may face difficulties relating to one another. For many, however, this is the best time in life. Couples have more freedom and disposable income, which allows for more leisure and social activities.

Growing in Faith during Middle Adulthood
The search for meaning and significance has brought many boomers back to church. They seek a moral compass to guide the rest of their journey. The key word to understanding this generation at the turn of the century is *balance*.

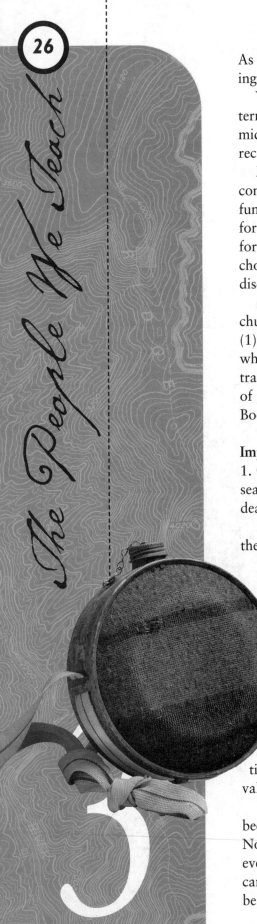

As boomers have aged, the drive to acquire possessions has shifted to improving the quality of life, which transfers to spiritual renewal.

When you listen to the prayers of middle adults, Father is their favorite term for God. They view the role of the Father as Teacher and Provider. As middle adults are called to provide for and teach the next generation, they recognize their dependence on Him as Teacher and Provider.

Middle adults often return to church during this period because of their concern for the spiritual growth of their teenagers. Parents want more than fun and games for their children. They seek—and demand—quality programs for their children. Boomers want relevant and meaningful worship experiences for themselves and for their teens. This generation has grown up with many choices, and they want the church to provide multiple choices for worship and discipleship opportunities

Gary McIntosh, in *Make Room for the Boom . . . or Bust,* believes the church can reach this generation of middle adults if the church becomes: (1) less stodgy and flexible enough to meet the real personal needs of Boomers who come to them, (2) sensitive to the needs of Boomers in areas outside of traditional spiritual concerns, (3) adaptable to giving Boomers a wide variety of participational choices, (4) responsive to the musical styles and tastes of Boomers, and (5) assertive in challenging Boomers to a great vision.[4]

Implications for Ministry with Middle Adults

1. Christian education must be developed with the conviction that there is a search for significance among middle adults and a desire to help individuals deal with these inner realities as well as the eternal events of life.

2. The church must be a community of faith that helps middle adults share the story of their faith with others.

3. Because they have more free time and fewer family tasks, middle adults should be viewed as prime candidates for leadership positions in the church.

4. Because of their concern for the nurturing of family life, middle adults are good prospects for teaching Bible study groups. This age group is also a good target for seminars and conferences that help adults be more effective fathers and mothers.

5. Middle adults who have satisfied the need for self-esteem are a counseling gold mine.

6. This age group could be the spiritual mentors to young adults.

7. Middle adults need to discover biblical truths that speak to existential questions such as: Why have I been placed here on this earth? and What values will I communicate to the next generation?

The discoveries and struggles of early and middle adulthood have only been prerequisite courses to more inviting challenges in late adulthood. Nothing that we have experienced will be lost or cast aside. Every road and every step of the way is preparation for new and greater journeys ahead. We can say with Robert Browning, "Grow old along with me! The best is yet to be, the last of life, for which the first was made. Our times are in his hand."[5]

Later Adulthood

As adults enter this stage of the journey through life, they will have more companions than ever. In 1960, 9.2% of the population of the developed world was over age 65. Today that figure has grown to 14.7 percent, and by 2010, adults over 65 will comprise 16.7 % of the population. Those figures will continue to swell until 1 out of every 4 adults is over age 65.[6]

At this period of life, chronological age becomes less helpful as a developmental guide to an adult's abilities and needs. Issues such as health, life and financial circumstances, and outlook on life play a more significant role. Besides, at what age are you *old*? Age is relative, depending on your perspective. To a 15-year-old, 30 seems ancient. To an 80-year-old, a 65-year old is still a youngster. Later adulthood is continually being redefined as medical technology, affluence, and advances in nutrition change the way we think about later years.

The current population of senior adults is the end of the Builder Generation. They built a country after the Great Depression, and fought and conquered Hitler. A courageous and loyal generation, they now are walking the later years of life. They are loyal to their denomination and committed to the ministries of the local church. They give liberally to the support of missions. Some members of the media appropriately have labeled them "The Greatest Generation."

The challenges facing this group's journey are no different in many ways than those facing other generations. This is the age of adjustment—adjusting to retirement and reduced income, to decreased physical strength and health, and to the loss of a spouse. Other challenges include establishing satisfactory physical living arrangements, meeting social and community obligations, and establishing explicit affiliation with one's age group. These challenges generally are viewed negatively, as signs of the approaching decline toward death. From a Christian perspective, the development tasks of later adulthood are not only predictable but also desirable because they mean growth.

SSFNC

Large, readable type encourages later adults to spend time reading and preparing their lessons before attending Bible study sessions.

Later adults face the evening of life with either a sense of integrity or a sense of despair. Despair is the inability to accept one's own life and death, thereby experiencing regret, frustration, and discouragement. Integrity is looking back on life with a sense of inner peace and the confidence that one's life had meaning and purpose, enjoying knowing that one made a difference in the world and contributed to the good of others. Those working with later adults can testify of friends who approach this stage with a sense of hope and wisdom, knowing that death is not the end, but a new beginning.

The Builder Generation is loyal to institutions. They understand commitment and sacrifice. Many churches would not survive without their financial support. This generation helped build most of today's churches and want to see their life's work continue. They are not necessarily opposed to change in church. Older adults will support change if they see that change makes a difference in the community and helps reach their grandchildren. Peter Peterson, a 72-year-old, says in his book *Gray Dawn,*

The People We Teach

I find most senior citizens to be far less selfish personally than the positions taken by their so-called advocacy groups. Most understand the moral imperative so clearly stated by Dietrich Bonhoeffer: 'The ultimate test of a moral society is the kind of world it leaves to its children.' Most seniors I know want a chance to contribute and a chance to make things better for their children and grandchildren. They are not opposed to sacrifice, but they want to know that any sacrifice they are asked to make is effective and fair.[7]

Many older adults will tolerate praise choruses and video clips in worship services if occasionally a familiar hymn is sung as well. However, if new approaches do not result in church growth, look for these adults to question the strategy and call for another approach.

Growing in Faith during Later Adulthood

The goal for those who have followed Christ in this journey through adulthood should be to arrive at the end of life mature, strong in character, full of wisdom, complete. Maturity and wisdom often are attributed to the elderly. Do the elderly have more mature faith than younger adults? Search Institute defines maturity as the integration of a life-transforming relationship to a loving God and a consistent devotion to serving others. The eight marks of a mature faith are:

1. Trusting and Believing
2. Experiencing the Fruits of Faith
3. Integrating Faith and Life
4. Seeking Spiritual Growth
5. Nurturing Faith in Community
6. Holding Life-Affirming Values
7. Advocating Social Change
8. Acting and Serving[8]

In its research, Search Institute found that "older churchgoing adults are more likely than younger adults to embody faith maturity. While only sixteen percent of adults in their twenties have an integrated faith, the percentage climbs to fifty-seven percent of people seventy or older."[9]

Where young adults view God as Friend and middle adults view God as Father, those in later adulthood have a more comprehensive, universal view of the Supreme. In the prayers of the elders, listen for the word Creator. God is Creator of the universe. He is sovereign. Everything is under His control. Nothing has escaped Him. Adults in their later years, look back on life and testify that God was with them every step of their journey.

Implications for Ministry with Later Adults

Older adults need to love and be loved. Earl Murphy tells the story of a woman who visited his Senior Adult Sunday School department for the first time. As was his custom, he gave her a hug. Murphy noticed that she grew stiff.

3

Recognizing her discomfort, he quickly pulled his arm away. They talked for awhile, then he continued through the group hugging and greeting everyone. For weeks, she continued to visit the church. He greeted her, but without the hug. One day, as he approached her she said, "You give everyone else a hug, why don't you give me one?" All of us need human touch. Senior adult self-preoccupation is fatal. Love for others and God is the only cure.

SSFNC

Bible study support resources include audiocassettes in Explore the Bible and Family Bible Study series.

Older adults need friends and companions. The importance of relationships in this stage of life should never be underestimated. Friends are of utmost importance to the life and health of seniors. Relationships with others, especially family relationships, are crucial for the development of personality. People become persons through relationships.

Senior adults need the support of others in dealing with the stresses of life. The number of homes with four generations under one roof grows annually. Adults in the early stages of later adulthood often find themselves sandwiched between generations. These retired—or nearly retired—adults find their time and finances redirected from leisure activities to providing for a parent who has come to live with them. The stress compounds when an adult child has "boomeranged" back home. Because of a broken marriage or job loss, the adult child needs a safe haven to get started again. While older adults will give up their time and life savings to care for their families, the mental, emotional, and physical stress can result in anger, bitterness, and physical exhaustion. Often carrying burdens like these alone, these Builders need friends and family who will lend a hand, pray for them, and encourage them through difficult times.

Older adults need to be useful. There is a wealth of experience, wisdom, and creative energy in the Builder Generation. There are still significant contributions this generation can make to the body of Christ. Leonardo daVinci produced the Mona Lisa in his 60s. Titian finished *Christ Crowned with Thorns*, considered to be his greatest work, when he was 82. Michelangelo created St. Peter's Church and frescoed the Pauline Chapel in his 70s and 80s. Imagine what masterpieces might yet be produced senior adults in your church. The body of Christ needs to find ways to use the spiritual gifts of the Builders.

Older adults need to have adequate resources for food, housing, and medical costs. Social Security, Medicare, and Medicaid will not be expected to keep up with the rising costs and bulging population of older adults. The church will have an excellent opportunity to demonstrate the love of God by assisting the elderly in the basic necessities of life. Some churches are making plans for retirement villages and assisted living facilities as part of their strategic plans.

Older adults have spiritual needs. Aging adults need assurance of God's continuing presence, protection, and provision. They need comfort in dealing with the fear of death and the loss of a loved one. The aging need the challenge of continued spiritual growth through Bible study. Older adults without Christ need to come to know Him. Through the FAITH Sunday School Evangelism Strategy® and other church evangelistic efforts, older adults are responding to the gospel of Christ.

The People We Teach

3

Adults in the evening of life need opportunities to express their understanding of God's provision. They provide a wonderful living testament to the grace of God. Collectively, they demonstrate the power of God at work in His people. They, like no others, have the experiential base to proclaim His goodness. As Linda Vogel declares in *Teaching and Learning in Communities of Faith*, "I believe that older adults should be the story bearers, as they are given encouragement and opportunities to share their faith stories. If we do not grasp this opportunity, these stories—and those of that generation's parents and grandparents—will be lost from the community memory."[10]

These stories of faith need to be collected and recorded for future generations to know these heroes of faith who are cheering them on.

Conclusion: The Journey Is Not a Solo Event

Sam Keen, in *The Passionate Life*, said: "The first question an individual must ask is 'What is my journey?' Only then is it safe to ask the second question: 'Who will go with me?' If you get the questions out of order, you will get in trouble."[11]

Yes, there are some who choose to backpack alone. But the really breathtaking views, such as Mount Everest or the Grand Canyon, require a team. God's grace, while experienced personally, can never be fully grasped alone. The apostle Paul wrote: "And I pray that you, being rooted and established in love, may have power, together with all the saints, to grasp how wide and long and high and deep is the love of Christ, and to know this love that surpasses knowledge—that you may be filled to the measure of all the fullness of God." (Eph. 3:17-19).

This passage has stumped many Christians. How can you know that which you cannot know? How can you know the full extent of a love that is beyond comprehension? The answer is found in the phrase, "together with all of the saints." The breadth of God's love is realized as we hear about the spilling out of His grace upon fellow pilgrims. No one adult can experience every act of God's love, but the church collectively does. You may not have experienced God's presence through the death of a child, the loss of a spouse, or financial difficulties, but many in the church have. As we hear their stories of faith, we begin to realize our God is an awesome God.

Spiritual growth is more than personal; it is communal. God conveys Himself to each of us not only through personal relationships with Him and our practice of spiritual disciplines, but also through other believers as we fellowship with them.

On a youth camping trip, one inner-city youth was alone by the fire. When I sat down by Erin, I noticed he was crying. I had never seen Erin cry. He was one of the toughest kids I had ever taught. "What's the matter, Erin?" I asked. Erin said nothing, but raked a piece of wood from the fire. We watched the embers turn from orange to white ash. After several minutes, Erin said, "I'm like that piece of wood. When I'm at church, I burn bright for Jesus. But when I'm away, I'm as cold as ash." What a perfect picture this is of the church. We need others to walk alongside us in the journey. We cannot go it alone.

Christian educators know that spiritual growth occurs best in small groups. This is where "family" happens, where you can share joys and sorrows. When you fall, others help you get up. As we minister to and with adults, we should pray words similar to those of Henri Nouwen, asking "the same Lord who binds us together in love will also reveal himself to us and others as we walk together on the road."[12]

Endnotes

[1]Dale G. Robinson, *Intersecting Lives: Road Maps for Ministry with Young Adults,* (Fresno, CA: Willow City Press, 1998), 39-40.

[2]Robinson, 36.

[3]Henry C. Simmons, "Human Development: Some Conditions for Adult Faith at Age Thirty," *Religious Education,* 71 (November-December 1976), 564-565.

[4]Gary L. McIntosh, *Make Room for the Boom . . . or Bust,* (Grand Rapids: Fleming H. Revell, 1997), 37

[5]Robert Browning, Rabbi Ben Ezra (1864), st. 1.

[6]Peter G. Peterson, *Gray Dawn,* (New York: Random House, 1999), 13.

[7]Peterson, *Gray Dawn,* 24-25.

[8]Eugene C. Roehlkepartain, *The Teaching Church,* (Nashville: Abingdon Press, 1993) 36-37.

[9]Roehlkepartain, 41.

[10]Linda Vogel, *Teaching and Learning in Communities of Faith,* (San Francisco: Jossey-Bass, 1991), 60.

[11]Sam Keen, *The Passionate Life: Stages of Loving,* (New York: Harper and Row, 1983), 172.

[12]Henri Nouwen, *In the Name of Jesus,* (New York: Crossroad, 1996), 42.

For Further Reading

Anderson, Neil T. & Saucy, Robert L. *The Common Made Holy.* Eugene, Oregon: Harvest House Publishers, 1997.

Browning, Robert. Rabbi Ben Ezra (1864), st. 1, in *Bartlett's Familiar Quotations,* 16th ed. Boston: Little, Brown, and Company, 1992.

Ford, Kevin Graham. *Jesus for a New Generation.* Downers Grove, Illinois: InterVarsity Press, 1995.

Hahn, Todd and Verhaagen, David. *GenXers after God.* Grand Rapids: Baker Books, 1998.

Keen, W. *The Passionate Life: Stages of Loving.* New York: Harper and Row, 1983.

McIntosh, Gary L. *Make Room for the Boom . . . or Bust.* Grand Rapids: Fleming H. Revell.

Peterson, Peter G. *Gray Dawn.* New York: Random House, 1999.

Robinson, Date G. *Intersecting Lives: Road Maps for Ministry with Young Adults.* Fresno, California: Willow City Press.

Roehlkepartain, Eugene C. *The Teaching Church.* Nashville: Abingdon Press, 1993.

Simmons, Henry C. *Human Development: Some Conditions for Adult Faith at Age Thirty,* Religious Education 71 (November-December 1976): pp. 564-565.

Stevens-Long, Judith and Commons, Michael L. Adult Life: *Developmental Processes, 4th ed.* Mountain View, California: Mayfield Publishing Company.

Vogel, Linda. *Teaching and Learning in Communities of Faith.* San Francisco: Jossey-Bass, 1991.

Daryl Eldridge is the Dean of the School of Educational Ministries at Southwestern Baptist Theological Seminary. He and his wife, Carole have two children, and reside in Arlington, TX.

Teaching Strategically

4

by Ross H. McLaren

Many people have the impression that being a Christian is merely a matter of "believing in Jesus" or "trusting Christ as my Savior." However, far more is involved in being a Christian. In fact, such thinking leads to shallow commitment and a lack of change in one's perspective on life and in one's lifestyle.

Spiritual transformation begins with a *change of heart*—"For it is with your heart that you believe and are justified" (Rom. 10:10). Spiritual transformation also includes a *change of mind*. In Romans 12:2 Paul urged his readers, "Do not conform any longer to the pattern of this world, but be transformed by the renewing of your mind. Then you will be able to test and approve what God's will is—his good, pleasing, and perfect will."

From Paul's statement we learn at least two important truths. First, there is a pattern to this fallen world and its assumptions, values, perspectives, and lifestyles to which we as human beings—whether we realize it—have become conformed. Second, our responsibility as believers is to consciously reject the pattern of this world and the living of our lives in conformity to it.

Our present assumptions, values, perspectives, and lifestyles are to be transformed into different assumptions, values, perspectives, and lifestyles that are in keeping with God's perspective on reality and His values. Such transformation comes from the renewing of our minds, a task that is continuous and progressive.

The Bible teacher is in a great position to facilitate the work of the Holy Spirit in bringing about this kind of transformation. As adults are exposed to the Bible in the context of a caring class, their minds and hearts become receptive to the truth of God's Word. They first discover that there is an authority beyond themselves with which they must deal. Then they begin to reflect on the differences between what they believe and what the Bible teaches. In time they are able to observe the practical application of biblical truth in the lives of others in the group. They begin to see that the Bible is relevant and really does apply to life! Without even realizing it, they are experiencing the transforming power of the Bible and God's Spirit.

The Holy Spirit is able to accomplish God's purposes with or without our help. God is sovereign and will do as He pleases. Still, He has chosen, amazingly, to work through His people. God can work through any Bible study regardless of the planning or teacher skill involved. However, God most often chooses to work through leaders who plan, prepare, study, and invest themselves in the important ministry of teaching the Bible. The wise teacher will approach teaching with forethought and intentionality.

How can transformational Bible teachers maximize their time in order to bring about the greatest change in the learners? The most effective teacher will begin with understanding that we all are driven by how we think. Transformation occurs as our thinking is changed from reflecting the patterns of this world to the patterns of God's Word.

The Patterns of This World

When Paul commanded the Roman believers, "Do not conform any longer to the pattern of this world" (literally, *of this age*), he was referring to the sin-dominated, death-producing realm characterized by the domination of sin and Satan, and from which Christ gave Himself to deliver us (Gal. 1:4). The verb Paul used for "conform" has the sense of forming oneself after another or of being formed like another. Thus Paul was referring to a conformity that follows a pattern, in this case the fallen world's pattern.

Paul warned believers against the power this fallen world exercises through social groups and institutions and cultural norms and traditions to mold character and individual patterns of conduct. In other words, Paul's command was a moral imperative.

Another way of saying "the pattern of this world" is to use the term *worldview*. Have you ever been in a discussion of a morally significant issue and, after you made a moral judgment or pronouncement, the person you've been talking with doesn't see it the same way? Then that person begins to tell you what he or she thinks. Why doesn't everybody see things the same way, especially important moral issues? The answer has to do with their worldviews.

A worldview, most simply, is the way a person views the world, or reality. More specifically, a worldview is the composite set of assumptions or presuppositions, beliefs, and values a person

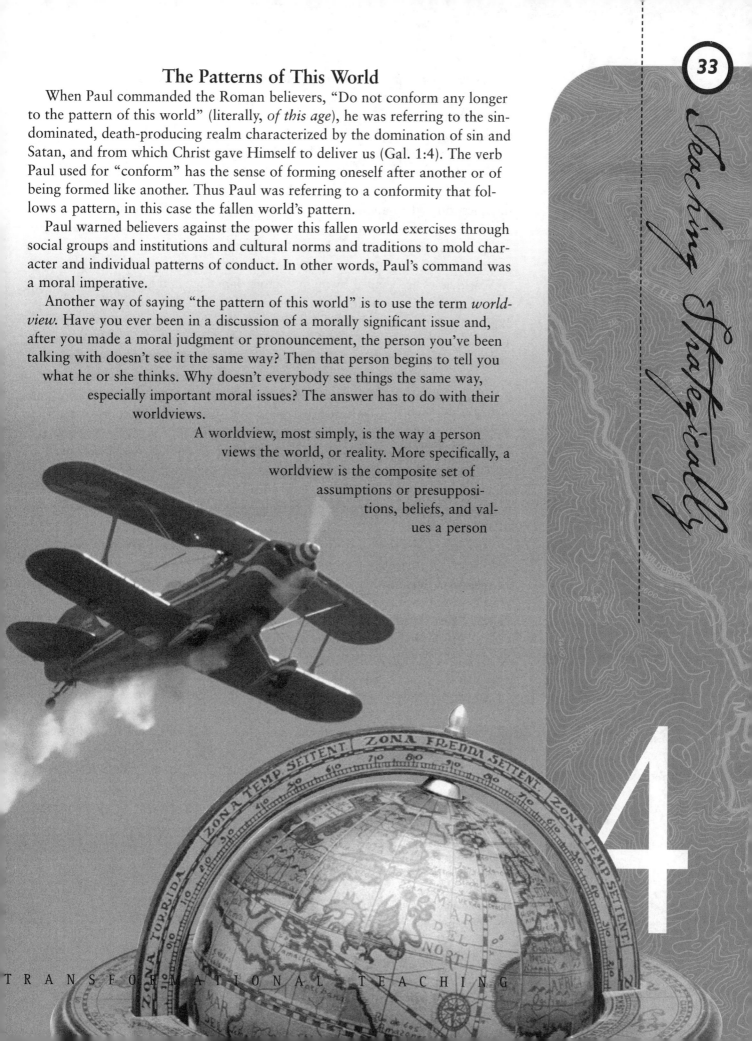

4

possesses—held consciously or unconsciously—that shapes how that person sees reality and determines how he or she will act. Thus a worldview not only is the lens through which a person perceives, interprets, and understands reality, but also provides the resulting value system that forms the basis for lifestyle choices. Further, a worldview is comprehensive. It filters all observations and covers all aspects of life.

Everyone has a worldview even though they may not know it. This raises the question, When and how are worldviews acquired? Worldviews are acquired early in life as a person absorbs or adopts the assumptions, values, perspectives, and lifestyles of his or her culture. This process is called *enculturation*.

Worldviews are shaped by many factors: language and geo-demographic factors, parental instructions and examples, family influence, and individual experiences in the world. Other factors include education and teachers, cultural institutions and customs, music and art, television and movies, peers and heroes, models and trendsetters, socio-political and religious institutions, proverbs and myths, rituals and taboos, as well as many other influences. Because societies, within certain boundaries, are bound together by a common view or way of life, worldviews are communal. This means that one tends to be unaware of his or her worldview and how it differs from other worldviews until that worldview is brought into comparison or conflict with other worldviews that challenge it. People not only acquire their worldview from their society, but also their worldview colors how they see and interpret their society. In other words, a worldview is both a view *of the world* and a view *for the world.*

How many different worldviews are there? In one sense, there are as many worldviews as there are people. In another sense, worldviews can be grouped according to various broader classifications. However different or similar people's worldviews are, at the most basic level there are two types of worldviews: Those developed by fallen human beings, and thus marred by sin; and God's, which He has revealed in the Bible.

Fundamental Life Questions

All people everywhere experience the passing of time. This is a universal experience. Not all people view time in the same way. Some people view time as a line moving from the beginning to the end. Others view it as a cycle. Regardless of how they perceive time in history, all people recognize the movement of time. Consequently, all people have a memory of the past, a consciousness of the present and some anticipation of the future. This is why all people have a "story." Each person's story will explain and determine his or her worldview.

When understood this way, it becomes apparent that each person's story and subsequent worldview is shaped by how he or she answers certain *Fundamental Life*

SSFNC

Relevant Life Questions identified for each session reflect the Fundamental Life Questions and help focus the lesson on pertinent adult issues. Questions can be used to reflect on God's Word and as discussion questions for use during the sessions.

Teaching Strategically

Questions. The question, Where did I come from? seeks to define the person's "prologue." What brought the individual to this particular point in the movement of time? The question, Where do I fit in? seeks to define the person's "story" or current situation. How we perceive our place in the world is defined by our relationships to people, places, and events in the world around us. The question, Where am I going? seeks to define the person's "epilogue." It tries to anticipate the future and how it will impact our lives.

In identifying these questions, keep two cautions in mind. First, Fundamental Life Questions may never be consciously articulated by an individual or a social group. Nevertheless, how one answers these questions—or what answers a person assumes to these questions—reveals the essence of his or her worldview.

Second, the forms in which the Fundamental Life Questions are expressed are temporally and culturally determined. That is, the Fundamental Life Questions may be asked in any number of ways or forms depending on one's language, place and time in history, socio-economic level, or background. Hence, what appears to be two different questions, with investigation, may prove to be alternative or representative forms of the same Fundamental Life Question.

Universal Life Needs

Each Fundamental Life Question gives birth to other questions that are more specific to life's circumstances. By analyzing the various ways people may ask these questions, we discover that the questions are universal because they are based on *Universal Life Needs* through which all of the rest of life and its experiences may be interpreted.

What are the Universal Life Needs people share and how many of them are there? While various models have been suggested, 12 life needs seem to be universally addressed in all worldviews.

1. Questions such as: What's real? Is there more to reality than meets the eye? How can I know that I know anything? and Can I really know what I believe is true? reveal that people need to have a plausible understanding of **reality and knowledge.**

2. Questions such as: Who or what has the power? Is there a god? and What is God like? reveal that people need to have a plausible understanding of **who or what has the power.**

3. Questions such as: Where did the world/we/my tribe come from? How did everything get started? and What is the nature of the universe? reveal that people need to have a plausible understanding of **origins.**

4. Questions such as: Who am/are I/we? Why am/are I/we here? and Am/are I/we important? reveal that people need to have a plausible understanding of their **identity and significance.**

5. Questions such as: What's wrong with the world? Why is there so much

suffering in the world? Why do bad things happen to good people? Why do people die? Do evil forces exist? Why does evil exist? and Why do I act the way I sometimes do? reveal that people need to have a plausible understanding of **evil, suffering, and death.**

6. Questions such as: Do we live on a dying planet? What can we do to ensure that the rain will fall and the crops will grow? and How can I make it through the night? reveal that people need to have a plausible understanding of **survival and security.**

7. Questions such as: What is truth? Is something true just because those in charge say it is? What should I/we believe? How can I/we know what's true when there are so many competing voices? Whom can I/we trust? and What's important and what's not? reveal that people need to have a plausible understanding of **truth and assurance.**

8. Questions such as: What's right and what's wrong? Is there a standard by which all people should live? How can I be good? and What should I/we do? reveal that people need to have a plausible understanding of **actions and behavior.**

9. Questions such as: Is there any way I can start over again? Is there any way I can make up for or undo past mistakes? Can I be delivered from the bondage I experience? How can I overcome feelings of alienation and estrangement? How can I be forgiven? and How can I be saved? reveal that people need to have a plausible understanding of **renewal and restoration.**

10. Questions such as: Does anyone care about me? How come nobody loves me? and Is there a place I can feel completely accepted and at home? reveal that people need **love and a sense of belonging.**

11. Questions such as: Who will I be? How can I be acceptable? How can I be important? How can I be great? and How can I find fulfillment? reveal that people need **fulfillment.**

12. Questions such as: Where are we going? Is there hope for something better than this? Are history and the universe heading toward a goal or is it all meaningless? Is this all there is? What happens to me when I die? Is there life after death? and Do you only go around once? reveal that people need to have a plausible understanding of **history's meaning, direction, and purpose.**

Transformation and the Renewal of the Mind

When Paul commanded the Romans, "Be transformed by the renewing of your mind," he used the Greek word *metamorphoo,* from which we get our English word *metamorphosis.* This same verb is rendered "transfigured" in the transfiguration narratives of Matthew 17:2 and Mark 9:2. The only other place in the New Testament where the word occurs is in 2 Corinthians 3:18, which speaks of believers being transformed into the likeness of Christ with ever-increasing glory. As with Christ's transformation in which His deity shone forth from

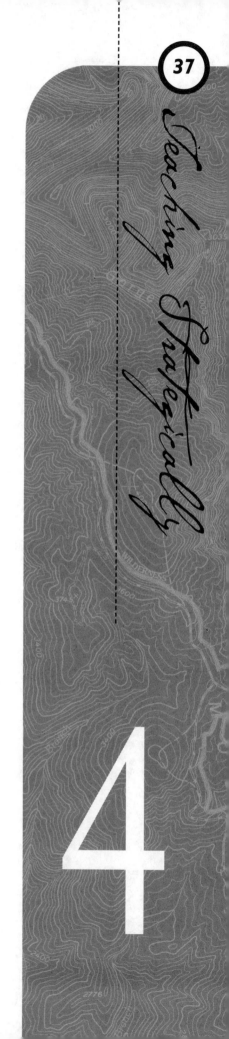

within, the word *metamorphoo* means to change one's outward appearance to agree with one's inner self.

The means by which this transformation is to take place is the renewal of the mind, or of one's whole way of thinking. The word Paul used for "mind" is *nous*. Twenty-one of the 24 New Testament occurrences of this word are in Paul's writings. It refers to the center of a person's thinking and reasoning, to one's way of thinking, to the center of a person's moral consciousness. Believers must adjust their ways of thinking about everything so that how they think matches God's views and values. As renewal takes place in the mind, a new way of thinking, a new worldview, and a new way of life will result.

Further, the verb "be transformed" is a present imperative. The present tense underlines the continuous nature of the renewal that is required in the new way of thinking and of living. Believers must work continuously and constantly at the transformation and renewal of our minds.

Developing a biblical worldview is not instantaneous. Such a worldview does not develop overnight. It is a lifelong process whereby the believer's worldview is transformed toward the divine or biblical worldview.

Biblical Worldview Categories

Only those who have adopted the biblical worldview share God's worldview, for having a biblical worldview is to think like God thinks and value what God values. This is what Paul meant when he added, "Then you will be able to test and approve what God's will is—his good, pleasing, and perfect will" (Rom. 12:2). Approving the will of God means to understand, agree with, and put into practice God's moral direction, that is, what God thinks and values.

Accordingly, as believers we must identify the basic elements of the biblical worldview and seek deliberately and systematically to integrate these into our lives and thinking. In doing so, we discover that because God made human beings, He has provided answers to the *Universal Life Needs* in what may be termed *Foundational Biblical Truths*. These truths comprise the basics of the biblical worldview and may be grouped into *Biblical Worldview Categories* that match specifically the universal life needs of human beings. These include:

1. **Reason and Faith.** God has addressed our need to understand the nature of **reality and knowledge.** The biblical worldview teaches us that reality is fixed and knowable. Reality involves both material substance and non-material or spiritual substance. In other words, there is more to reality than meets the eye. Much of what can be known is gained by reason, but faith lays hold of reality and knowledge that is not accessible to the senses.

2. **The Person and Nature of God.** God has addressed our need to understand **who or what has the power.** The biblical worldview teaches us that Jehovah God is the only true God. He is personal, all-powerful, sovereign, transcendent, eternal, unchanging, and triune. God is holy, just, kind, good, gracious, and loving. He is the creator of all that is, both visible and invisible.

God is the source of all life. He acts out of love, grace, and compassion and desires the best for His creation.

3. **Creation.** God has addressed our need to understand the mystery of our **origins.** The biblical worldview teaches us that creation consists of both material or physical elements and immaterial or spiritual elements. God's creation functions with order, predictability, and splendor. God has established natural laws according to which the universe operates.

4. **Humanity.** God has addressed our need of **identity and significance.** The biblical worldview teaches us that all people are created in the image of God and are, therefore, valuable as individuals. Human beings are total entities consisting of a material body and an immaterial spiritual part. God made human beings male and female. He gave them an equality of status but a difference of roles. As the creation of a personal God, people possess personality, intellect, creativity, self-consciousness, and self-determination. Humanity's highest purpose is to love God and worship Him. Human beings are responsible to be good caretakers and stewards of God's creation. Even though everyone has fallen into sin and rebellion against God, through faith in Christ individuals can have their true humanity restored. Therefore the identity and significance of individuals is found in his or her being in the image of God by creation and by being in Christ by redemption.

5. **Rebellion and Sin.** God has addressed our need to understand the meaning of **evil, suffering, and death.** The biblical worldview teaches us that rebellion of cosmic proportions has occurred in God's creation. Both spirit beings and human beings have rebelled against Him. All human beings have sinned against God. Because all have sinned, everyone is fallen and lost. The relationship between God and every person has been broken. Sin has resulted in alienation, condemnation, enslavement, depravity, and death. Creation itself suffers from the impact of sin and is, therefore, no longer as God created it.

6. **Sovereignty and Providence.** God has addressed our need for **survival and security.** The biblical worldview teaches us that God is sovereign over His creation. Nothing occurs without His permission. God is at work in the world. He actively continues to preserve, provide for, and sustain His creation. He providentially controls, guides, and directs the universe and history toward His desired end, despite all hindrances. God preserves the stability and order of the natural realm through natural laws. He works through His natural laws to renew His creation's resources and to meet the on-going needs of humanity. God preserves the stability and order of the social realm through the bonds of marriage and family, the rule of law, and stable civil government.

7. **Revelation and Authority.** God has addressed our need for **truth and assurance.** The biblical worldview teaches us that God has revealed Himself in many ways—through nature, conscience, and special acts, including Scripture and Jesus Christ. God has spoken objectively, personally, and propositionally. His revelation is intelligent and intelligible, true and trustworthy, authoritative and final. Because it is God who has spoken in the words of the Bible, the Bible is authoritative in all that it affirms, teaches, and commands. Hence, the Bible has the authority to command our beliefs and order our behavior.

8. **Ethics and Morality.** God has addressed our need to know how to **act and behave.** The biblical worldview teaches us that God is a holy God. He is the moral standard by which all moral judgments are measured. God created human beings with a moral nature and has established moral absolutes. As such, humans are moral agents who are morally responsible to God. Human beings have both personal and social moral obligations. God has revealed His moral standards through human conscience, Scripture, and the witness of the Holy Spirit. Human beings, therefore, are responsible for abiding by creation ethics and Christian ethics.

9. **Covenant and Redemption.** God has addressed our need for **renewal and restoration.** The biblical worldview teaches us that God was not thwarted by the rebellion of His creation. He has chosen to call into being a covenant people whom He blesses and restores. God initiated this blessing under the old covenant and will fulfill it under His new covenant, which was inaugurated by Jesus Christ. God's covenant is an act of divine grace and calls for fidelity on the part of His people. God has acted in history to redeem human beings and His creation through His Son, Jesus Christ. In Jesus Christ, God entered into time and space in human form, and He suffered and died to atone for sin in the place of (as a substitute for) human beings. This is the basis of the hope of redemption. God offers forgiveness of sins and reconciliation to those who will trust in Christ's sacrifice. To them, God promises hope, resurrection, and victory.

10. **Family, Community, Church, and Kingdom.** God has addressed our need for **love and a sense of belonging.** The biblical worldview teaches us that God made people to need other people. God ordained the family, communities, societies, and nations to accomplish His purposes in our lives through love, discipline, encouragement, and security. Believers discover their purpose and identity in relationship to their families, the people of God, the fellowship of Christ's church, and the realm of His kingdom.

11. **Discipleship and the Christian Life.** God has addressed our need to find **fulfillment.** The biblical worldview teaches us that believers achieve greatness through being transformed into the image of Jesus Christ and by giving themselves to His service and ministry. The Christian life is a life of discipleship that involves self-denial, obedience to God's commands, vigilance in prayer, an authentic witness, cultivation of the mind of Christ, production of the fruit of the Spirit, progression in holiness, demonstration of Christian virtues, and perseverance in faithfulness. Growth in Christ is characterized by an awareness of the positional nature of redemption and the completed work of Christ in the life of the believer.

12. **Time and Eternity.** God has addressed our need to discover **history's meaning, direction, and purpose.** The biblical worldview teaches us that God is not limited by time. He works within time to accomplish His purposes. The

Teaching Strategically

Bible presents a progressive view of time. Time is moving forward meaningfully and purposely because God is moving time, history, and creation toward a determined end. Someday Jesus will return in power and great glory to raise the dead, judge the world, punish the lost in a place called hell, reward the redeemed in heaven, establish His kingdom, renew heaven and earth, and consummate His redemptive mission.

Strategic Bible Study

While all believers are responsible to cultivate the biblical worldview in all areas of their lives, as finite creatures people will never fully reach the point where they possess the complete mind of the infinite God on all matters. Nevertheless, Christians are to grow toward possessing a worldview that is increasingly biblical.

SSFNC

Life Impact statements help both leaders and learners understand the difference the session's biblical truth should make in their lives.

The process of embracing and living according to the biblical worldview involves a lifetime of Bible study, conscious reflection, attitude adjustments, mental scrutiny, mature guidance, and lifestyle changes. This underscores the need for Bible study that is strategic and deliberate. Transformational Bible teachers should approach Bible study strategically. That is, they should view teaching as part of a long-term ministry or strategy. Teaching God's Word is more than a series of single lessons. Teaching is an opportunity to move learners, over time, toward specific theological goals, toward the biblical worldview.

Strategic Curriculum Design

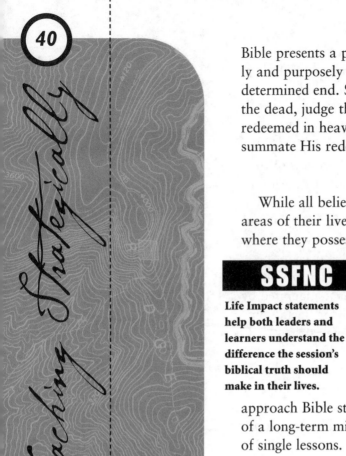

Many resources are available to help leaders move learners toward the biblical worldview. One of the most overlooked and undervalued resources is dated curriculum materials. Dated curriculum materials assume an ongoing approach to the Bible study context. Consequently, dated materials approach Bible study holistically and strategically. The dated Bible study approach is strategic because it provides several important characteristics.

Scope—Scope refers to the limits of acceptable subject content. In a Bible study group, the scope is the Bible itself. A strong dated study plan for adults will ensure that all of the Bible is covered appropriately in a reasonable amount of time.

Balance—Most parents understand the value of a balanced diet for their children. Balance also is important in Bible study. Good dated study plans will lead learners to explore God's Word in a balanced approach to its content. This will mean a balance of studies from both the Old and New Testaments, teaching passages balanced with narrative passages, etc.

Sequence—Sequence refers to the order of studies over time. A well-sequenced dated study plan will move learners toward carefully planned unit goals. In addition, the dated study plan will take into account important seasonal factors like Christmas, Easter, and so forth.

Time—One of the most strategic features of dated curriculum materials is the simple way the study approach makes use of time. Dated study plans can take years to accomplish certain goals. There's no need to cram everything into a few sessions.

Context—Dated Bible study takes place most often in the context of an ongoing Bible study group. As people form relationships in an ongoing group, they are able to see how the truth of God's Word is working in the lives of other learners. This context alone provides a strategic advantage to dated curriculum resources.

Strategic Bible study may be the teacher's best tool as he or she intentionally attempts to inculcate all aspects of the biblical worldview into the hearts and minds of people. God has entrusted these learners to you so that they may become more like Christ as they are transformed into His likeness.

Strategic Curriculum Choices

The use and choice of Bible study curriculum is a strategic decision that should be made carefully and deliberately. This choice will determine the "diet" of Bible study your learners will receive. Good choices in curriculum will help move your learners toward the biblical worldview.

Bible study group leaders typically can choose from either dated or undated curriculum resources. Both kinds of resources offer distinct advantages to a church's curriculum planner. Dated curriculum resources typically offer a plan with stronger scope and sequence, as identified above. Undated resources, however, often provide a stronger "hook" for groups hoping to appeal to non-participants on the basis of the study's topic. Dated resources typically work well in an ongoing Bible study group while undated resources work quite naturally in a short-term group.

SSFNC

Dated Bible study plans address each of the Biblical Worldview Categories. Information regarding dated Bible study plans is available by logging onto www.lifeway.com/sundayschool.

A church's curriculum planner should consider the strengths and weaknesses of both dated and undated resources. Planners also should consider the nature of the group in choosing curriculum materials (see page 50). For example, open, evangelistic Bible study groups will want to avoid resources that assume all participants are believers.

The bottom line is that leaders making these decisions for their churches should do so *intentionally* and *strategically*. They should avoid choosing solely on the basis of what sounds attractive. A Bible study topic may get someone in the door, but it's usually the relationships and ministry environment that bring them back. Sooner or later, believers need access to a healthy diet of Bible study in order to help them develop a worldview that is biblical.

Ross H. McLaren is Biblical Studies Specialist, Adult Sunday School Ministry Department, LifeWay Church Resources, Nashville, TN, and attends Primera Iglesia Bautista, Nashville, TN, where he attends an Adult Sunday School class.

Paths Toward Transformation

5

by Judith A.
Wooldridge

As I turned from one state highway on to another in rural Tennessee, I questioned my passengers about our road choice. Even though it didn't feel right to any of us, we chose to follow the tiny compass in the car's rear window. Because that compass continued to indicate east or southeast, I knew I probably was going in the right direction. Soon I found a place to pull off the road and check a map. The decision to trust the compass had been right. Even though we had gone too far south, we still were where we needed to be to get home.

Travelling the roadway toward spiritual transformation can be much like wandering physical highways without consulting a map or a compass. We think we can accomplish spiritual growth and maturity on our own. Just as the compass and map provided the evidence needed to find the way home, there are principles we can follow that will lead us home spiritually. These principles, which appear quite self-evident like the compass and the map, ultimately lead us to follow our true Guide who will take us down the paths to spiritual transformation.

Principle 1: Use the Bible

The Bible reveals God's nature, His expectations of people, His plan for redeeming people, and His instructions for living according to His plan. The Bible, which is the authoritative guide for all of life and the textbook for spiritual transformation, leads people to know God, both intellectually and experientially. Its historical accounts show God's involvement and intervention in the lives of people while its ethical teachings indicate how people are to live in relationship to God and others. The eschatological portions of Scripture reveal our future in Him. The Bible points us to the power, majesty, and work

of God. The proper human response to that revelation is loving, trusting, and obeying Him, as shown in these two passages:

All Scripture is God-breathed and is useful for teaching, rebuking, correcting and training in righteousness, so that the man of God may be thoroughly equipped for every good work (2 Tim. 3:16).

For the word of God is living and active. Sharper than any double-edged sword, it penetrates even to dividing soul and spirit, joints and marrow; it judges the thoughts and attitudes of the heart (Heb. 4:12).

In Isaiah 55:11, we find God's promise that His Word "will not return to me empty, but will accomplish what I desire and achieve the purpose for which I sent it." Even seemingly contemporary and relevant religious studies cannot claim this kind of empowerment.

In 2 Timothy 2:15, Paul told Timothy that teachers and leaders must also learn to use the Bible properly. Paul gave testimony in 2 Corinthians 4:2 that neither he nor those who taught with him distorted God's Word. Both biblical accounts point to how important it is for teachers to practice sound biblical principles of interpretation.

The value of this principle must not be overlooked by the transformational Bible teacher. Whatever resources you may use other than the Bible, you primarily must use the Bible in your teaching if you wish to see the simple power of God's Word impact your learners. Don't let anything become a substitute for the Bible.

SSFNC

Printed Bible passages in learner and leader guides point to the biblical message. Explanatory comments related to the focal and background passages assist leaders and learners in discovering the meaning and context of passages for the original hearers as well as for readers today.

Paths Toward Transformation

5

Principle 2: Depend on the Holy Spirit

The Holy Spirit is at work in God's world convicting people of sin and drawing them to God (John 16:8-11). The Holy Spirit is present in believers, revealing spiritual truth and enabling them to understand this truth, discern its application to their lives, and become transformed people. The spiritual transformation of lives occurs only through the Spirit's power.

SSFNC

The weekly personal Bible study in leader guides encourages Young Adult and Adult Sunday School leaders to reflect personally on the Bible study lesson, to depend on the leadership of the Holy Spirit in the preparation process, and encounter the truth of the Bible study before leading learners to encounter that truth.

The Holy Spirit is both active and essential in spiritual transformation, serving as the Teacher, Guide, and Empowering Agent. While selected theories of secular education are useful in Christian education, adherence to secular theories alone will not achieve spiritual transformation. Bible teaching for spiritual transformation begins with teachers who pray and depend on the ministry of the Holy Spirit.

How the Holy Spirit transforms lives is beyond human understanding and beyond human power to accomplish either in one's own life or in the lives of others. Review the biblical evidence.

"And I will ask the Father, and he will give you another Counselor to be with you forever—the Spirit of truth. The world cannot accept him, because it neither sees him nor knows him. But you know him, for he lives with you and will be in you.   . . . But the Counselor, the Holy Spirit, whom the Father will send in my name, will teach you all things and will remind you of everything I have said to you" (John 14:16-17,26).

"When the Counselor comes, whom I will send to you from the Father, the Spirit of truth who goes out from the Father, he will testify about me" (John 15:26).

"But I tell you the truth: It is for your good that I am going away. Unless I go away, the Counselor will not come to you; but if I go, I will send him to you. When he comes, he will convict the world of guilt in regard to sin and righteousness and judgment: in regard to sin, because men do not believe in me; in regard to righteousness, because I am going to the Father, where you can see me no longer; and in regard to judgment, because the prince of this world now stands condemned. I have much more to say to you, more than you can now bear. But when he, the Spirit of truth, comes, he will guide you into all truth. He will not speak on his own; he will speak only what he hears, and he will tell you what is yet to come. He will bring glory to me by taking from what is mine and making it known to you" (John 16:7-14).

"When the day of Pentecost came, they were all together in one place. Suddenly a sound like the blowing of a violent wind came from heaven and filled the whole house where they were sitting. They saw what seemed to be tongues of fire that separated and came to rest on each of them. All of them were filled with the Holy Spirit and began to speak in other tongues as the Spirit enabled them. . . . Peter replied, 'Repent and be baptized, every one of you, in the name of Jesus Christ for the forgiveness of your sins. And you will receive the gift of the Holy Spirit'" (Acts 2:1-4,38).

While following the back-road pathways, I trusted my hunch as well as the compass and the map. While walking the pathway toward spiritual transformation, human hunch is inadequate. We must depend on a power to transform our lives that is beyond our human understanding or ability—the Holy Spirit. To be used of God in teaching to transform lives, we first must be transformed ourselves and live in dependence on the power of the Holy Spirit.

Principle 3: Teach God's Word in and Through the Family

Even though personal Bible study is enriching and fulfilling for the individual, teaching people the Bible requires more than self-fulfillment—a teacher must live in relationships with the learners. The home is the first place where Bible teaching for spiritual transformation should occur.

Deuteronomy 6:6-8 calls for parents to instruct their children in, through, and around the home. Proverbs 1:8-9 calls on children to listen as both father and mother instruct them. One of the best known proverbs, Proverbs 3:5-6, offers instruction for a son to trust in the Lord and not lean on human understanding.

The New Testament speaks specifically to family relationships and responsibilities. In 1 Peter 3:1-7, Peter addressed the roles of husbands and wives. Peter's instructions first to Christian wives and second to Christian husbands include in verse 7 an assumption that a husband and wife will spend time together in prayer. Contemporary couples can use the Bible to study together, share together, and build their time together in prayer.

Priscilla and Aquila, a married couple, dedicated their lives to instructing others in God's Word. Acts 18:24-28 describes an occasion when the couple heard Apollos, a learned man who spoke with "great fervor" but had an incomplete understanding of Jesus. Priscilla and Aquila "invited him to their home and explained to him the way of God more adequately." In similar fashion, people today have used and can use their homes as a base for leading people to faith in Christ and instructing them with God's Word.

In Ephesians 6:4, Paul clearly stated the principle that fathers should take the lead in bringing up their children "in the

SSFNC

Learner guides stress the importance of spending time together in the Bible as a family. Some young adult and adult learner guides offer daily, interactive Bible study elements with one that can be utilized weekly with the family. Other adult learner guides promote weekly preparation for Bible study and utilization of printed devotional resources, both of which can be family activities. Young adult and adult leader guides provide helps for the leader in encouraging the importance of family Bible time and offer occasional follow-up suggestions in the "Continue" section.

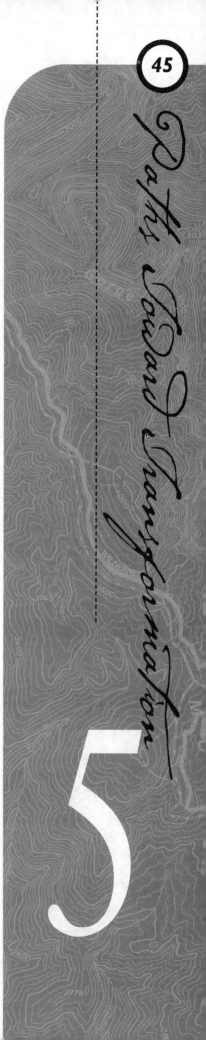

training and instruction of the Lord." In 2 Timothy 1:5 Paul magnified the role of teaching God's Word within the context of the family by affirming Timothy's grandmother Lois and his mother Eunice for their roles in laying the foundation for Timothy's faith. Then in 2 Timothy 3:15, Paul reminded Timothy of how teaching and learning the Scriptures from infancy within his family had led Timothy to the time when he placed his personal faith in Christ.

My parents taught me the importance of following a compass and a map while in unknown territory. In the same way, parents have the primary responsibility in the religious education of their children. It is imperative that our Bible teaching sessions with young adults and adults and the resources used before, during, and after those sessions support and encourage spiritual growth and understanding within the context of the home. Your teaching can never replace the responsibility carried by the family. Always be looking for ways to partner with the family in your teaching.

Principle 4: Magnify Relationships with the Learners, Wherever You Gather Them

Commissioned by Jesus Christ and empowered by the Spirit, a church is to teach people to know and understand God's Word as well as challenge them to obey it and appropriate the Word into their own lives. Spiritual transformation through Bible teaching can occur within the fellowship of a church as people interact with one another in the presence of the Holy Spirit through groups that facilitate relationships. According to Acts 2:41-47, the Christians in Jerusalem not only repented, believed, and obeyed in baptism, they also practiced mutual prayer. Note in the following list the impact on Jerusalem when God's Word was taught and obeyed within the context of strong relationships:

• filling of everyone with awe
• doing of wonders and miraculous signs by the apostles
• giving to anyone with a need
• eating together with glad and sincere hearts
• praising God
• enjoying the favor of all the people
• the Lord's adding to their number daily those who were being saved

Who wouldn't want to be a part of a group of people who were so transformed!

A ministry of teaching God's Word has the power to transform lives from spiritual lostness to spiritual life. Therefore, teaching God's Word in varied places—apartment complexes, office settings, campus religious or Bible study groups, any place people can be gathered—is a powerful strategy to fulfill the Great Commission given to us in Matthew 28:18-20.

Paul's willingness in Acts 17:16-34 to go public to instruct the philosophers at the Areopagus in Athens might appear to serve only to add to the frustration and loneliness he felt in a city "full of idols." Paul understood he had to discover how to relate his teaching to his hearers if he was going to reach their philosophical minds. Paul creatively referred to their "unknown god" (v. 23) and quoted their poets (v. 28). Some of the hearers sneered when Paul mentioned the cornerstone truth of the Christian faith—Jesus' resurrection. However, as Paul left the meeting "a few men became followers of Paul and believed . . . also a woman named Damaris, and a number of others" (vv. 33-34).

The principle is clear: Teaching people God's Word bears fruit when the instructor relates to the people in language, terminology, and concern enough to be creative. To use Paul's own words in 1 Thessalonians 2:6b-8: "As apostles of Christ we could have been a burden to you, but we were gentle among you, like a mother caring for her little children. We love you so much that we were delighted to share with you not only the gospel of God but our lives as well, because you had become so dear to us." In order to instruct others in such a way that God transforms lives, teachers not only must connect to the learner's head but also to the learner's heart.

Just as I received instructions I could understand and identify with as a child about a compass and a map, we must learn to communicate the biblical message in that same manner with people of all ages. We also are responsible for connecting that knowledge to the hearts of our learners. Spiritual transformation occurs in both the head and the heart. However, this cannot occur unless leaders engage learners in meaningful relationships that foster growth and focus on individuals.

Principle 5: Hold Teachers and Other Leaders Accountable

Accountability is a biblical principle. Teachers and other leaders need to be held accountable in some way for at least the following actions.

Model spiritual transformation. A teacher's spiritual transformation is the beginning point of the spiritual transformation of Bible study group participants. A teacher is also a learner, particularly when he or she follows the example of Jesus, who modeled all He wanted to communicate. John 13:15 records Jesus' words, "I have set you an example that you should do as I have done for you."

Bible teaching moves beyond words. Teachers must live what they teach. Teachers communicate more by their lifestyles than by their words. In Luke 6:40 Jesus cautioned His disciples, "A pupil is not above his teacher; but

SSFNC

Leader guides provide teaching helps for small-group activities that encourage growth in relationships either through the group dynamic of the learning activities themselves or through suggestions that evolve out of the activities. Leader guides also include ideas for a leadership meeting's focus on relationships as well as ministry-type articles that challenge leaders with the relational needs of learners and with ideas for building relationships within a small group.

Paths Toward Transformation

5

everyone, after he has been fully trained will be like his teacher." Paul identified in his writings the principle that learners imitate their teachers and also used it as a principle for teaching (1 Cor. 1:11; 1 Thess. 1:6-7; Phil. 4:8-9).

Teach people God's Word. In the Great Commission, Jesus commissioned all believers to teach others to obey all that He said. The Holy Spirit endows some individuals in a church with special teaching gifts. Yet any believer can be called to teach. A teacher is to teach for change, creating an environment and guiding learning in ways that facilitate the work of the Holy Spirit and encourage the spiritual transformation of learners (Matt. 28:19-20; Acts 15:35; Eph. 4:11-13; Col. 3:16; 2 Tim. 2:2; James 3:1). A teacher committed to teaching for change recognizes the ways learners learn best as well as their levels of learning (1 Cor. 3:1-2; Heb. 5:11-14; John 16:12).

Build people. A teacher is a leader. All leaders are responsible for living as authentic witnesses of Jesus Christ. As a leader, a teacher is accountable for building people by strengthening relationships with and among Bible study group participants, leading lost people to saving faith in Jesus Christ, being certain that people are cared for, and developing new leaders/teachers for service through a church's ministries.

Once in my childhood, we turned down a back road I could not find on the map I held in my hand. I questioned my father about it, but he told me not to worry and identified which road he thought we soon would intersect. I was quite impressed when he was on target with his prediction. Later he explained that he judged our direction based on the sun, on the time of day, and on where we were when we turned onto the road. Not only was he teaching me by letting me follow on the map, he also modeled good judgment in his own actions. As teachers and leaders with young adults and adults in Bible study groups, we also must model good judgment in how we follow the Holy Spirit's work in our personal lives, in how we teach for spiritual transformation, and in how we develop new leaders.

Principle 6: Lead Learners to Be Accountable

Not only do teachers and leaders need to be held accountable, learners also need to be held accountable for the following things. It is our responsibility as leaders to teach and lead in such a way that calls for this kind of accountability from learners.

For their spiritual transformation. All people—preschoolers, children, youth, young adults, or adults—learn in different ways and on different levels. It is vital that a

SSFNC

Leader guides offer leadership meeting suggestions and a "Prepare" section, which encourage leaders to work together and to be accountable for personal preparation.

SSFNC

Some young adult and adult learner guides call for learner accountability through daily interactive Bible study features after the session. Other adult learner guides focus on studying the lesson before the session. Suggestions in the "Continue" section of leader guides offer leaders ideas for encouraging learners to be accountable for both learning and living transformed lives.

learner accepts a growing responsibility for learning as a faithful follower of Christ (1 Pet. 1:5-11). Each individual is responsible for allowing the Holy Spirit day-by-day to transform him or her to become more like Jesus Christ. Learners should study God's Word with teachable hearts and obey the Holy Spirit's leadership (Rom. 6; 12:1-2; Eph. 4:20-24; 5:8-10; Phil. 3:7-14; Col. 1:9-12; 1 Pet. 1:13-16).

For sharing their lives with others. Learners can teach one another, particularly by sharing their stories of how God is working in their lives (1 Thess.2:8). Not only is each believer important for the effective work of the church, each believer also is responsible for involvement in evangelism, discipleship, fellowship, ministry, and worship.

Principle 7: Engage in Evaluation and Reflection

Because of their strategic roles of influence, teachers "will be judged more strictly" (Jas. 3:1). In addition to being accountable for examining themselves and their faith, teachers also are accountable to their learners and should seek to understand their learners' learning styles and progress toward spiritual transformation. Not only should teachers evaluate how well they achieve the teaching objectives of specific lessons, but also they should evaluate their effectiveness in their spiritual transformation goals of leading people to faith in Christ and guiding people to grow in Christlikeness.

Regular leadership meetings offer a prime opportunity to evaluate and reflect on the effectiveness of Bible study groups in reaching people for Christ. No matter how well leaders feel they have done in teaching people the Bible, the key test comes in how well the Bible study group has done in "drawing the net" or assimilating unsaved people into the group and introducing them to the gospel. In addition to making these evaluations in a leadership meeting, leaders must take careful stock of themselves before participating in an overall evaluation.

SSFNC

Leader guides offer weekly leadership meeting helps, quarterly ministry articles, and a "Life Impact" statement for each lesson that can be used as a week-by-week evaluation tool.

Yes, we did arrive back home from our journey through the back roads. A compass and a map reminded me that I could not find my way on my own. In the same way, being spiritually transformed personally and teaching others for spiritual transformation cannot be accomplished on one's own. The Bible and the Holy Spirit provide us with the tools we need for teaching God's Word in and through our families, for magnifying relationships with learners, for being accountable leaders, for leading learners to be accountable, and for evaluating and reflecting on our spiritual transformation.

Judith A. Wooldridge is Senior Product Development Specialist, Adult Sunday School Ministry Department, LifeWay Church Resources, Nashville, TN, and coteaches a Bible study group of single adults at Springfield Baptist Church, Springfield, TN.

Teaching in a Group

"The Lord God said, 'It is not good for the man to be alone. I will make a helper suitable for him.'"
Genesis 2:18

With these simple words, God summed up the social nature of the human being He had just created. We all need companionship. This need for companionship moved God then to create the first family or community.

When God pronounced judgment on the serpent after the fall, He promised One who would crush the serpent's head. This One would come through the seed of the woman. This was a promise that could be fulfilled only in the context of family and community. Since that time, God has worked consistently through a community or group to accomplish His redemptive purpose.

The Scriptures most often assume that God's Word will be taught in the context of a group or community. The group may be large or small. The idea of one-on-one Bible teaching is neither a bad one nor foreign to the Scriptures, but is not, however, the most typical approach. This book assumes that your teaching involves a group of adults.

Understanding the Group's Purpose and Nature

The purpose of a Bible study group will greatly influence how teachers teach the Bible. That's why teachers must articulate the group's purpose at least for themselves if not for the group as a whole. In addition to assuming that you are teaching several people who make up a group, this book also assumes the group is, by design, a "Bible study group." A Bible study group is a group intentionally formed around the study and living of God's Word. That is at least part of its primary purpose.

The informal teaching of God's Word can take place rather naturally and spontaneously in almost any group. Comments made at lunch or riding in the car can effectively communicate biblical truth, but these groups are not Bible study groups. This is also true of many of the legitimate groups that exist within the church. Biblical truth is regularly "taught" in the choir, for example, but the choir is not a Bible study group.

6

by Rick Edwards

There are different kinds of Bible study groups. For our purposes, we will consider two important characteristics; the group's *nature* and the group's *duration*. The group's nature refers to the group's basic intent or purpose. The Bible study group's nature can be one of two different kinds, either open or closed. The group's duration refers simply to how long the group intends to exist. Duration can be either ongoing or short-term.

These labels—open, closed, ongoing, short-term—are intended to be descriptive and may not reflect what any given church calls their Bible study groups. Your church may use terms like *Sunday School class, cell group,* or *small group.* The label isn't as important as the group's purpose and nature.

Open Bible Study Groups

Open Bible study groups typically are always open to new people joining the group. Sunday School groups should be open groups. Other groups may or may not be open, depending on the group or church's leadership. Some of the strengths of open Bible study groups include:

- Open Bible study groups tend to foster relationships with the family of God and within the family of God because participants help newcomers feel wanted, welcome, and expected. This open nature exposes learners to a variety of people with a variety of needs and maturity levels. This diversity usually helps the group assimilate people and build relationships rather than focus on skill development.
- Open Bible study groups support the church's evangelism function because they typically seek lost people to participate in the group. Leaders and Christian learners alike will pray for, plan for, and hope for lost people to be present in the Bible study.
- Accountability placed on the learners for lesson preparation is typically a basic level in an open group. If newcomers are welcome at any time, then requiring advance preparation or former study is not practical. Newcomers, lost people, and guests must be made to feel welcome anytime in an open Bible study group.

The teacher in an open group must recognize that a newcomer may be present in any given session. This newcomer may not bring any significant Bible knowledge to the session, either. This newcomer may not be a believer or even possess a Bible. Yet, the teacher of an open group must be prepared to lead a meaningful and challenging Bible study for all participants. (The next chapter will explore this aspect of teaching more thoroughly.)

Closed Bible Study Groups

Closed Bible study groups typically are limited to those individuals who have made a particular commitment or demonstrated a particular need. Closed Bible study groups may be open for the first session or two, but then become closed at some point. Groups aimed at leadership training, skill development, or discipleship are examples of closed groups. Some of the strengths of closed groups include:

- Closed Bible study groups tend to focus on functions within the body of

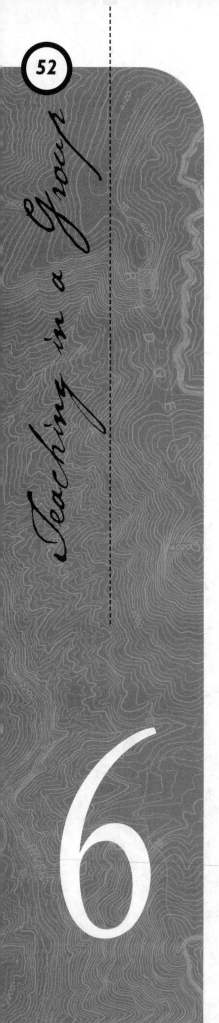

Christ because they have a limited scope of participants with no expectation of newcomers. Spiritual growth, maturity, and skill development are typically the priorities for this kind of group, as opposed to intentional assimilation and relationship building.

- Closed groups support the church's discipleship function because they can limit participation to believers and expect more from participants. Membership or participation in the group may be limited to only Christians or even Christians with a certain discernible commitment level.
- Accountability placed on the learners typically is higher in a closed group. This enables the group to "go deeper" in its study. A higher level of maturity or commitment may be expected or even required so that learners understand the need for home or supplemental study.

These study groups usually are closed to allow group participants to focus more intensely on a particular topic or issue. Closed groups enable learners to develop a set of skills, understanding, knowledge, or experience as each study builds on prior material.

The teacher of a closed Bible study group is challenged with the need to "stay ahead" of the learners. A certain degree of pre-existing skill or understanding typically is expected of teachers of closed Bible study groups.

Because the group is closed, the teacher has the opportunity and responsibility to become better acquainted with each participant. Relationships always play an important role in transformational Bible teaching, but closed Bible study groups typically provide a strong opportunity to know each learner.

Ongoing Bible Study Groups
Ongoing Bible study groups are those with no intention of ending at a particular date or time in the future. Some of the strengths of ongoing groups include:

- Ongoing Bible study groups can be closed or open, though they tend to be open more often because of attrition that occurs over longer periods of time.
- Ongoing groups do a good job of supporting the church's fellowship function when they allow relationships to develop naturally over a long period of time. They provide a long-term environment for building lasting friendships.
- Ongoing study groups emphasize the church's long-term obligation and commitment to discipleship and biblical instruction.
- Ongoing study groups focus initially more on purpose, member development, and relationship building rather than topics of study or affinity needs of the group.
- Ongoing study groups allow for long-term study plans that can provide greater balance, stronger sequence, and more comprehensive scope over time.
- Ongoing study groups typically meet around the time for corporate worship, which is convenient for participants and reinforces the essential relationship between worship and education.
- Ongoing Bible study ministries normally offer a fully age-graded ministry, solving a number of child-care issues. A fully age-graded ministry provides a

stronger family ministry by offering substantive, age-appropriate Bible study for all family members.

- Ongoing Bible study groups typically are easier to maintain for the church leadership. This is true for several reasons:
  ✔ These groups tend to have a more permanent location, time, and facilities.
  ✔ Leader enlistment typically is annual rather than every few weeks.
  ✔ Materials typically are dated and ordered rather automatically.
  ✔ Materials usually are less expensive.
  ✔ Record keeping most often is centralized and easier to administer.
  ✔ Study content usually is determined by the publisher rather than church staff.

For the transformational Bible teacher, the greatest advantage of ongoing Bible study groups is the simple time factor. Teachers of ongoing groups have the advantage of taking the long view and knowing that it takes time for people's convictions and perspectives to change.

The ongoing Bible study group teacher should think of every Bible study session as a meal he or she has prepared for the learners. The individual meal is not as important as the overall diet that the learner shares. This can free the teacher to focus on a single, important truth, rather than feeling the need to communicate everything in every session.

Short-term Bible Study Groups

Short-term Bible study groups simply are groups that have a specified start and/or end date. They do not intend to go on indefinitely. Some of the strengths of short-term groups include:

- Short-term groups, like ongoing groups, can be either open or closed, though they tend to be closed because they typically have a specific agenda to cover in a fairly narrow amount of time.
- Short-term groups also can support the church's fellowship function when they seek to establish relationships based on participants' needs.
- Short-term groups often meet in homes where a more informal and intimate environment can be created.
- Short-term groups often appeal to unreached people who will not attend a group at the church or are designed to meet for an indefinite period of time.
- Short-term group study content can be selected to appeal to individuals with very specific life needs.
- Short-term groups are not limited by public building space.
- Short-term group leaders can be enlisted more easily sometimes because of the shorter-term commitment.
- Short-term groups tend to focus more intentionally and naturally on building relationships from the outset because participants often are there with something in common.
- Short-term groups often develop a clearer sense of focus and intentionality

because the group's leaders know precisely where the group is going from the beginning and know exactly how long it has to get there.

Short-term Bible study group teachers must be very focused and deliberate. Time is limited. The teacher must have clearly defined goals in mind for the course as well as each individual session. Teachers must resist the temptation to communicate everything they know about all subjects.

Teachers of short-term Bible study groups must recognize the challenges they face in their efforts to bring about genuine transformation in learners. All of the elements of teaching for transformation become more critical as the time available is shortened.

SSFNC

Bible study resources help Adult Sunday School leaders and learners stay focused on the broader mission of the group—evangelism, discipleship, fellowship, ministry, and worship—while encouraging spiritual transformation and personal involvement in the Bible teaching ministry of the local church.

A church should be intentional and strategic in how it uses each kind of group. Each of these kinds of groups interact or relate to the others in some way. Leaders should develop a strategy that builds on the strengths of each kind of group. A comprehensive strategy that includes all four kinds will do the best job of reaching, assimilating, and building strong believers.

Sunday School Groups

The principles of transformational Bible teaching that are found in this book will apply to any Bible teacher. Most of those studying this book, however, will be traditional Sunday School class teachers. If that's true for you, you will want to know where you fit in to this whole discussion. How can you understand your group so you can be the best possible teacher for your learners?

Adult Sunday School for a New Century defines Sunday School as the foundational strategy in a local church for leading people to faith in the Lord Jesus Christ and for building Great Commission Christians through Bible study groups that engage people in evangelism, discipleship, fellowship, ministry, and worship. The local church is, of course, free to define their Sunday School ministry any way it wishes. If, however, the church affirms this definition, then that means the Sunday School teacher in that church is leading an open Bible study group.

Most Sunday School groups are ongoing, open Bible study groups. They are, theoretically, open to newcomers at any time and they have no specific end date. If this is true for you, then you have an exciting opportunity to influence both lost and saved people over a long period of time. Some Sunday School groups may be short-term, but they should always be open.

There are five strategic principles that help define and guide the church's Sunday School strategy and any given Sunday School group. Each of these has implications for how you teach your group.

Foundational Evangelism. Sunday School is the foundational evangelism strategy of the church. Because it is foundational, it is not everything the church will want to do regarding evangelism. Still, Sunday School is the best long-term approach for building a ministry environment that encourages unsaved people to come to faith in Christ, assimilates new believers into the life of the church, and encourages believers to lead others to Christ. This means you should teach with a sensitivity to lost people who should be present in the session. Are you considering the needs and condition of lost people when you prepare and lead the session? More will be said about this in the next chapter.

Foundational Discipleship. Knowing God through Jesus is the first step of discipleship. Sunday School is a seven-day-a-week strategy for involving people in seeking the kingdom of God and fulfilling the Great Commission. It is not everything the church will want to do to disciple God's people, but it certainly provides foundational discipleship as it gathers Christians to study the Bible. This places a heavy responsibility on both you and the church to see that Christian learners in your group are provided with a balanced diet of Bible study over the long haul. Are you taking the long view of teaching with your learners? Are your learners getting a balanced diet of Bible study?

Family Responsibility. Sunday School affirms the home as the center of biblical guidance. Bible teaching should always affirm and never usurp the role of the family in biblical instruction. Bible study is for all ages. Sunday School, therefore, provides an excellent strategy for engaging the entire family in meaningful, age-appropriate Bible study. Are you encouraging the parents in your group to strengthen their families? Are you encouraging a family Bible time that relates to the group's Bible study?

Spiritual Transformation. Sunday School affirms that God is working to transform His people through a new identity in Christ and a lifelong relationship with Him. Transformational Bible teaching must go beyond the "dispensing" of knowledge in order to foster this new identity, encourage the learner's personal relationship to Christ, and challenge the inner convictions that drive the learner's behavior. Do you know if your learners are Christians or not? Do you understand the inner issues your learners are facing so you can teach with relevance? Are you learning the basic convictions that drive your learners in their actions and behavior?

Biblical Leadership. Sunday School calls leaders to follow the biblical standard of leadership. Each teacher is accountable before God for the responsibility God has given him or her. Personal Bible study, ministry, prayer, lesson preparation, and evangelism all help leaders develop strong skills. Are you seeking to become the biblical leader God desires for you to be? Are you accepting the spiritual responsibility that comes with being a Bible teacher? Are you willing to invest the energy and time it will require to be what God desires?

Rick Edwards is Director of the Adult Sunday School Ministry Department, Sunday School Group, LifeWay Church Resources, and an adult teacher at First Baptist Church, Hendersonville, TN.

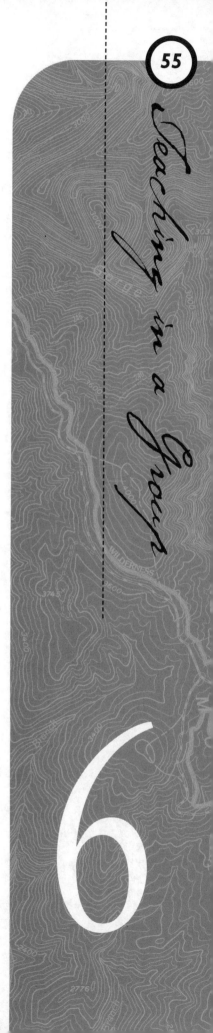

6

Teaching an Evangelistic Group

7

by Rick
Edwards

"Assemble the people—men, women and children, and the aliens living in your towns—so they can listen and learn to fear the Lord your God and follow carefully all the words of this law."
Deuteronomy 31:12

God has always drawn a distinction between His people and those outside of His family.

The Old Testament refers to those outside the community of faith as "aliens." The Mosaic law excluded aliens from participation in certain worship and ritual observances. The New Testament also reflects this difference between God's people and all others. Paul wrote: "The man without the Spirit does not accept the things that come from the Spirit of God . . . and he cannot understand them, because they are spiritually discerned" (1 Cor. 2:14). The Bible is clear that there is a difference between the child of God and the individual who is not. The person who has not established a faith relationship with God is lost.

At the same time, God encouraged His people to include the "alien" when it came to hearing, understanding, and observing His Word. The passage that began this chapter highlights God's admonition that the alien hear His message. That passage also sets forth the broader missionary heart of the Father. God always has desired to expand His family and His kingdom. His promise to Abram was to bless "all peoples on earth" through his descendants (Gen. 12:3). God's loving heart has not changed all these centuries later.

Understanding Evangelistic Bible Study Groups

In chapter 6 we explored Bible study groups: open groups, closed groups, ongoing groups, and short-term groups. Open groups always are open to new people joining the group. This openness will include people who are lost and need Christ. An open Bible study group is, therefore, evangelistic by its nature. That is, open groups are designed for lost people to participate so they can be saved.

It's important to note the distinction between an evangelistic group and a group with evangelistic people in it. For example, a short-term Bible study group for deacons theoretically will be filled with believers who desire lost people to get saved. We would hope that these deacons are active witnesses and seek daily to win people to Christ. So, the people in the group are, hopefully, evangelistic. The group itself, however, is intended only for deacons and is, therefore, not evangelistic. However, the study group itself does not intend to win people to Christ. It is closed and limited to only deacons.

An evangelistic Bible study group understands that winning people to Christ is part of its purpose. Evangelism is one reason for its being. Guiding people to Christ is part of the group's nature. Evangelistic Bible study groups historically have been amazingly effective evangelistic tools for several reasons.

Evangelistic Bible study groups allow lost people to build natural relationships with believers. Through these relationships, lost people discover that in many ways, they are much like their Christian friends. Christians struggle with the same issues in life that unbelievers experience. Lost adults need to see that maturing in Christ is a growth process and that each Christian is at a unique level of maturity. Non-Christians need to experience God's grace and love through the believers in the class. As this happens, they begin to feel more comfortable with God's family and the community of faith. In time, most will desire the same spiritual devotion and power.

> ### SSFNC
>
> **Articles in the Ministry Resources pages and in leader and learner guides in general support evangelism and encourage adults to become effective personal evangelists through their Bible study groups. Each curriculum series also provides at least one evangelistic lesson each quarter.**

Evangelistic Bible study groups provide a non-threatening environment in which lost people can explore the claims of Christ and the God of the Bible. To some, the paths of Christian beliefs are clouded, dark, and seemingly hard to navigate. Lost people have honest questions about the Bible and Christianity. They typically have been heavily influenced by a secular and anti-biblical worldview that makes the claims of Christ sound unreasonable or silly.

As lost adults study the Bible, they can ask their questions and voice their concerns in the context of a group that has demonstrated concern for them as individuals who are important to their Christian friends. They can be honest about their doubts. In time, the Spirit of God and the power of God's Word will influence their thinking. Christianity will begin to sound reasonable, not silly.

Evangelistic Bible study groups create a Christian support system for unbelievers in times of crisis. When an open group functions properly, members of the

group take seriously the need to care for all people in the group. Sooner or later we all will experience some kind of crisis or need. Sometimes we will enjoy celebrating some experiences of life with friends and family. At times we will need people to care for us. This is true for unbelievers as well. When crises happen, an open and evangelistic Bible study group can be there to provide encouragement, concern, sympathy, food, babysitting, prayer, hand-holding, money, cleaning, laundry, yard work, or any number of other means of support.

Evangelistic Bible study groups guide lost people to the power of God's Word. Bible teachers must always keep in mind that the Bible is no ordinary book. The Bible is the objective Word of God, inspired by Him and empowered by His Spirit. Isaiah 55:11 reminds us that God's Word will not return to Him "empty." God promises that it "will accomplish what I desire and achieve the purpose for which I sent it." Consistent exposure to this amazing book will help a lost person sense the heart and love of God and experience His conviction, forgiveness, and blessing.

If finding and leading the lost to Christ is a priority for the local church, then church leaders must take seriously the tremendous potential and historic effectiveness of evangelistic Bible study groups. Churches should be strategic and deliberate in their planning, promoting, and use of these kinds of groups.

Teaching an Evangelistic Group

In one sense, people are people. We share certain characteristics that reflect both the image of God and the impact of sin. We all struggle with fundamental life questions and experience similar needs. Yet there is a spiritual difference between a believer and a lost person. How does someone who teaches adults balance the needs of believers and unbelievers in a Bible study group? How do teachers meet the spiritual needs of lost people while helping believers grow in their faith? The process begins with some basic understandings.

Lost people can study the Bible. All people have been created by God and bear His image. Thus lost people are able to read the Bible and understand, to some degree, both the message and context of biblical passages. The Bible is like a compass that helps people find direction, in particular toward God. When God spoke through the objective words of the Bible, He spoke both intelligently and intelligibly. That is, He spoke words, sentences, and passages that had specific meanings. They were intelligent. God intended for these passages to communicate to humanity. He did not speak words that mean something only to Him. They were spoken to humankind and are, therefore, intelligible.

Because God has spoken in a way that people can understand, it is reasonable to assume that lost people can understand the messages God conveys through His words. This does not mean that they'll be able to understand the Bible at the same level or with the same impact as a believer. A note written from a husband to a wife often will communicate more than someone outside the relationship may discern. Still, the teacher of an evangelistic Bible study group needs to recognize the capacity lost adults have to study the Bible in meaningful ways.

If lost people can study the Bible, then teachers of evangelistic Bible study groups should not be afraid to engage lost adults in a challenging exploration of God's Word. We shouldn't be afraid to deal with tough questions. Unbelievers have brains too. They want, need, and deserve to see that Christianity is a reasonable faith that deals honestly with serious life issues. Some of history's greatest and most influential thinkers have been unbelievers. They can challenge us and sharpen our beliefs. Their presence in a Bible study group can energize the study and challenge all learners to think more seriously about their own faith.

Relationships are most critical. In the final analysis, people are not looking merely for intellectual answers to life's questions. People need people. They need and seek relationships. They search for love, acceptance, affirmation, and a sense of belonging. They need more than a comfortable mind; they also need a comfortable heart. Geniuses need love too!

Lost people especially need meaningful relationships. They have never experienced God's forgiveness. They don't know what being loved unconditionally by the sovereign, creator God feels like. But most want to be loved that way. A caring Bible study teacher can reflect that love and help lost adults see how God's grace can make a difference in their lives. In most instances, the love of people in the group lays a foundation for lost people to come to Christ. The Holy Spirit can use that foundation of love and friendship to help the lost experience God's love.

The priority of relationships means that teachers of evangelistic Bible study groups should be willing to go beyond the session to build relationships with unbelievers. One-on-one conversations over coffee or dinner can remove many barriers lost people may have built to the gospel. It's natural for newcomers--both believers and unbelievers--to bring a certain level of skepticism to the group. As teacher and learner get better acquainted, the walls that hinder learning will come down. A deepening relationship also will help the teacher know how to direct the Bible study session. Understanding each learner's unique circumstances can help the teacher be more relevant and meet a learner's particular needs.

Integrity is essential. As a rule, lost people don't expect believers to be perfect. They do and should expect, however, for a Bible teacher to approach the study and the group with integrity. Our culture has made all of us more skeptical about our leaders. We have difficulty believing that what we see is what we get. We wonder if the people we meet in the routines of life are genuine and real. We want to know that those who lead us are real.

Integrity doesn't mean perfection. It does mean, however, that a person is not pretending to be one thing while actually being something else. Believers and unbelievers alike understand the need for integrity, but integrity is especially important for Bible teachers who desire to teach lost people and win them to Christ.

The Bible provides real answers to real life problems because God's Word is true and real. The Bible teacher must communicate that God's Word can be trusted. A genuine and honest spirit in the teacher can go a long way toward helping lost adults believe the Bible is relevant and true. The teacher of an evangelistic Bible study group should be willing to share his or her own struggles and failures. A transparent life can go a long way toward demonstrating integrity. It shows that you struggle with life just as lost people do. Transparency shows that

Teaching an Evangelistic Group

teachers sometimes fail just like other people fail. Perhaps most importantly, it shows lost adults that their leaders can be honest about those failures.

Initial impressions are lasting. Sometimes we forget how we felt when we joined a new group. We have become so comfortable with our own Bible study group that we think everyone will be as comfortable with the group as we are. We forget that a newcomer or guest often knows nothing about anyone in the group. We forget how important first impressions are for newcomers. We somehow forget the Golden Rule when guests attend our Bible study group.

Sooner or later, all evangelistic Bible study group teachers should visit a comparable kind of group in another church in which they are not known. Leaders should go prepared to take notes. They should record their impressions as they go along. Were they made to feel welcome when they arrived? Did they have to sit alone for even a few moments before the session began? How did it feel to be a guest? What should they do differently in their group based on their experience? This can be an amazingly productive exercise and open a teacher's eyes to the needs of a lost person attending the group for the first time.

Relevance makes the difference. Many things compete for the attention of those who attend a Bible study group. This is really true for lost people. Many believers will be motivated factors that reflect a sincere commitment to Christ. Lost people, however, must find the Bible study relevant and meaningful. Relationships can be established almost anywhere. The workplace or a local nightclub can provide a place to meet people and build friendships. In order for lost people to find a Bible study valuable, the session must address real life needs faced by real life people.

The need to provide a relevant Bible study session can present the teacher of an evangelistic Bible study group with an interesting challenge. On one hand, some believers in the group may desire Bible study that focuses on searching the biblical content. They may enjoy exploring the rich depths of God's Word and want to know what the Bible says. On the other hand, unbelievers want to know why what the Bible says matters. How does the Bible apply to life? They want to know the so what of Bible study!

The competent Bible teacher will seek to balance life application with biblical content. In addition, teachers must lead believers in the group to see the need to avoid Bible study that addresses content without application.

Planning for evangelistic Bible study will help. Most Bible teachers are diligent students of God's Word and take their teaching responsibility very seriously. They study, plan, and prepare for hours before teaching. Even experienced teachers can prepare without giving adequate attention to the evangelistic side of their teaching. Like most things, we do what we plan to do. If we don't plan an evangelistic Bible study, then we probably won't lead one.

Planning for evangelistic Bible study is really pretty simple. The best thing to do is simply to think about how the study should be changed by the presence of someone who is lost. If a teacher knows particular lost people who will be present, it's even easier to tailor the session to be sensitive to them. This doesn't mean every session must include the plan of salvation as part of the study. It does mean that every activity and application should be considered in advance to determine whether it is appropriate for a person who is lost. The real key here is sensitivity.

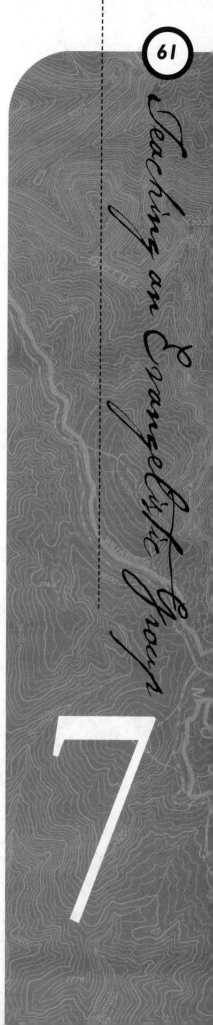

Keeping an Evangelistic Group Evangelistic

More than any other single person, the teacher will set the evangelistic tone and heartbeat for the group. This places a significant burden on the teacher to instill within believers a desire to see the group reach people for Christ. How can the teacher keep the group evangelistic?

Be unapologetic and open about the group's purpose. Use every opportunity to remind the group that one of the reasons the group exists is to win the lost to Christ. There's no need to hide or apologize for wanting to bring people out of the spiritual wilderness of sin and lead them along paths of faith and spiritual growth. If we really believe lost people are going to hell, then love compels us to tell them.

Celebrate victories when a lost person of the group gives his or her heart to Christ. This can be as simple as reporting the event for the sake of the class. The class may wish to stand with the person when someone makes a profession of faith. Members certainly will want to be present when the new Christian is baptized. Celebrating will communicate to participants that people getting saved is important to the group.

Encourage learners to invite lost guests to all activities, especially fellowship events. This reminds them that even fellowship activities are not just for them and aren't just for fun. Avoid activities that are not open to guests or lost people.

Use nametags for everyone. This communicates to members that they need to be sensitive to newcomers. Those who are resistant to nametags usually become supportive when they see the value of nametags to guests and lost newcomers. Nametags provide a weekly opportunity to remind the group of its purpose.

SSFNC

The leader guide assumes the group desires to reach people for Christ and that lost people may be present in any given session.

Pray for lost people, even by name when appropriate. Voicing a prayer for lost individuals will highlight the reality of a spiritual battle. Learners will be reminded of the priority of evangelism.

The Sunday School Challenge

Sunday School groups historically have been evangelistic Bible study groups when they functioned properly. When placed in their historical perspective, Sunday School groups have been one of the most effective tools ever used for evangelism in the church. Unfortunately, many Sunday School groups have forgotten why they exist. Rather than remaining open to and seeking lost people and maintaining a heart for evangelism, many groups have become closed and focus more on those attending than those whom they should be reaching.

The time has come for Bible study teachers to be challenged to rekindle the fire of evangelism in their own hearts and in the groups they lead. The challenges can be great, but the rewards are eternal and please the One who has saved us and called us to have an evangelistic heart.

Rick Edwards is Director of the Adult Sunday School Ministry Department, Sunday School Group, LifeWay Church Resources, and an adult teacher at First Baptist Church, Hendersonville, TN.

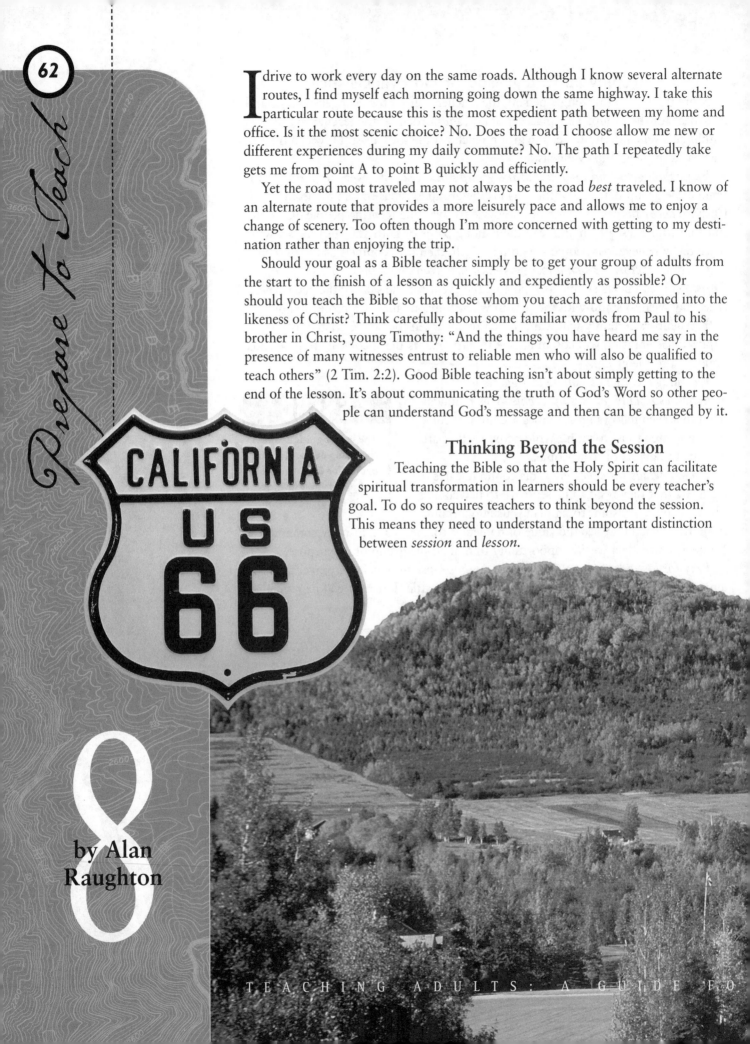

8

by Alan
Raughton

I drive to work every day on the same roads. Although I know several alternate routes, I find myself each morning going down the same highway. I take this particular route because this is the most expedient path between my home and office. Is it the most scenic choice? No. Does the road I choose allow me new or different experiences during my daily commute? No. The path I repeatedly take gets me from point A to point B quickly and efficiently.

Yet the road most traveled may not always be the road *best* traveled. I know of an alternate route that provides a more leisurely pace and allows me to enjoy a change of scenery. Too often though I'm more concerned with getting to my destination rather than enjoying the trip.

Should your goal as a Bible teacher simply be to get your group of adults from the start to the finish of a lesson as quickly and expediently as possible? Or should you teach the Bible so that those whom you teach are transformed into the likeness of Christ? Think carefully about some familiar words from Paul to his brother in Christ, young Timothy: "And the things you have heard me say in the presence of many witnesses entrust to reliable men who will also be qualified to teach others" (2 Tim. 2:2). Good Bible teaching isn't about simply getting to the end of the lesson. It's about communicating the truth of God's Word so other people can understand God's message and then can be changed by it.

Thinking Beyond the Session

Teaching the Bible so that the Holy Spirit can facilitate spiritual transformation in learners should be every teacher's goal. To do so requires teachers to think beyond the session. This means they need to understand the important distinction between *session* and *lesson*.

The session is that specific period of time when your group meets to study the Bible. This may happen on Sunday or any other time of the week. Whenever your class or study group meets, the session has a definite beginning and ending time.

The lesson is that particular Bible truth that God desires to convey to those participating in the session. Time or place does not determine or limit the lesson! The session then becomes one of many ways to communicate the lesson.

Three Essentials of Transformational Teaching

When teachers recognize the distinction between the session and the lesson they will begin to think beyond the session and seek to "teach" the lesson before, during, and after the session. To do this, they'll need to utilize the three essentials of transformational Bible teaching: **Prepare, Encounter,** and **Continue.**

Before the teaching session, you **prepare** the ministry environment for spiritual transformation. During the session, you guide the learners toward spiritual transformation through an **encounter** with the Word of God in a Bible study group. After the session, **continue** to guide your learners toward spiritual transformation in daily living and family relationships as they struggle with the truth and decide whether to believe and obey. This chapter will focus on **Preparing** for the session.

Preparing a Ministry Environment

Effective Adult Bible teachers do not just breeze over the Bible passage and waltz in to teach life-changing lessons. Transformational Bible teachers create an environment for ministry that enhances Bible study. By creating such a ministry environment, they enable the Holy Spirit to move beyond teaching Bible content to leading adults toward spiritual transformation.

The ministry environment is more than just the physical facility. It is everything that relates learners to the group and to one another. It is the total context of the group's work and mission. It is largely relational and recognizes that transformation always occurs in the context of a caring community of faith.

This kind of ministry environment doesn't happen by accident. It happens when leaders pray for, plan for, and work for it to hap-

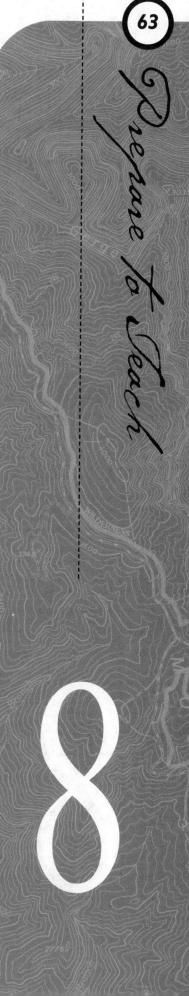

8

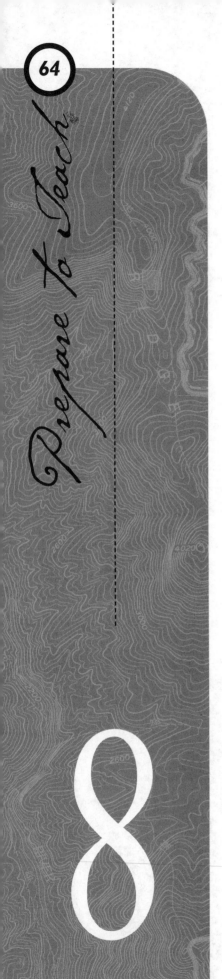

pen. You can prepare such a ministry environment in two ways, leadership meetings and personal Bible study.

Leadership Meetings

The building of a ministry environment is a challenging task. The wise Bible teacher will recognize the value of working with other leaders to create the desired atmosphere, processes, and activities essential to any ministry environment. This cooperation with other leaders will provide numerous benefits.

- Encourages and strengthens adult leaders.
- Strengthens outreach and evangelism.
- Improves administration.
- Promotes stronger team spirit.
- Encourages evaluation.
- Improves coordination and communication.
- Improves teaching.
- Increases involvement in Bible study sessions.
- Makes better use of space and equipment.
- Calls attention to enrollment and attendance goals and reports.
- Leads to greater involvement in the work of the church.
- Provides for ongoing training.[1]

Regardless of schedule, a leadership meeting has some common content.

General Period (15 min.). This period is a brief gathering of all Bible sudy group leaders under the direction of the leader administering the Bible study ministry. The purpose of the general period is to motivate and inform leaders in areas of concern to the whole Bible study ministry.

SSFNC

Ideas and suggestions for use in weekly leadership team meetings are included in leader guides.

Department/Class Leadership Meeting (60 min.). This period is the primary focus of the weekly leadership meeting. Each of the following segments is to contribute to the achievement of the purpose of the Bible teaching ministry. Instead of a segmented prayer period in which prayer tends to become generic, prayer is to permeate the discussion in each area of work. This will allow for more specific and focused praying about issues and people.

- Focus on Mission—This portion of the meeting relates the work of the Bible teaching ministry to the mission and the ministry of the church. Information is shared concerning the church's ministry. Leaders are made aware of churchwide emphases, needs, and concerns, and how Bible study groups can support them.

- Focus on Relationships—During this time, relationships are discussed, individual needs assessed, and plans made to involve members in responding to needs. Approaches are determined for being involved with learners beyond the session. Specific plans are made for following up on ministry needs of members and prospects. Plans are made for fellowship activities and various assimilation actions to involve learners in loving and caring relationships. In an evangelistic Bible study group, visitation assignments and reports can be shared. Churches using FAITH Sunday School Evangelism Strategy® can use this time to review assignments, make reports, and make follow-up assignments. Occasionally, a study and review of witnessing approaches may be conducted at this time.

• Focus on Bible Study—Teaching for spiritual transformation is facilitated when leaders work together to plan the best way to bring learners into a life-changing encounter with the Bible message. Bible study is not seen as an independent task but is the focal point around which the group meets. During this time, previous Bible study sessions may be evaluated, assignments made, and plans determined for how to teach Bible content in subsequent sessions.

SSFNC

EXTRA! is a set of online tips teachers can access by logging onto the Adult Sunday School website at www.lifeway.com/biblein-sites.

Personal Bible Study

Participation in a leadership meeting is not enough to prepare you to teach adults. Personal, individual Bible study is indispensable to transformational Bible teachers. Spending time with the Lord, engaging in personal Bible study, and depending on the Holy Spirit means teachers are preparing personally for God to use them to teach His Word.

Personal Bible study doesn't begin with asking about learners. It begins with you, their teacher. You must explore God's Word and let it speak to you first. Before beginning, pray and submit to the lordship of the sovereign God. This is how you individually acknowledge your need to let Jesus Christ control your heart, mind, and life.

Once you have prepared your own heart, you'll want to approach the Bible text by doing three things: Observe. Interpret. Apply.

Observe the Scripture Text. Observing the Scripture text will help you capture the passage content. Try to determine what God was saying to the first readers or hearers. Read the text several times. Try reading it from several different translations. Read it until it's easy to read. Read it aloud. Listen for voice inflections and emphases.

As you read, ask: What, where, when, why, and how kinds of questions. This will force you to slow down and help you discover who is writing to whom, where they are, when it occurred, what is going on during this time, what they are to do, why the author is writing, and how they are to do what they were instructed to do.

As you read the passage, you will notice certain words or phrases being repeated throughout. If there are several different words of phrases being repeated, mark each one of them in a distinctive way so you can quickly see which one is repeated the most. Review each marking and if you learn a specific truth about that repeated word or phrase, record what you learn on a separate piece of paper in list form using words directly from the text. This will give you a compilation of truths you've gleaned about that subject.

Look for the main message. Some passages may have more than one key point. Make sure you understand the main thing the writer was attempting to communicate in the verse or verses being read. The list of truths you created from the marked words and phrases often will reveal the main message. The main message typically is the subject that was discussed the most.

As much as possible, observe the passage before reading commentaries or other helps on the text. If you don't understand it at first that's okay. Guess at the mes-

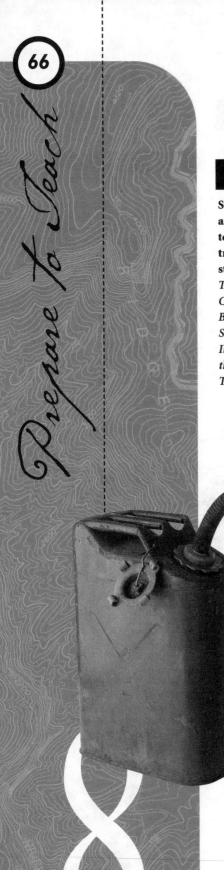

Prepare to Teach

sage if you have to. Don't fear being wrong. God wants you to understand His Word. He is pleased with your effort even if you fail to understand the text at first.

Be sure to ask the Holy Spirit to teach you, lead you, and guide you as you read the Scripture. He wants you to understand what you are reading. Wrestling with the passage on your own by observing the text will become a rich exercise for you.

SSFNC

Supplemental resources are available to help teachers prepare for transformational Bible study. Resources include *The Herschel Hobbs, Commentary, Advanced Bible Study Commentary, South Truths, Biblical Illustrator,* and *Explore the Bible Adult Cassette Tape.*

It is here that the "mystique" of the Bible begins to fall away so you can read it as it was intended to be read. The Bible is a special book with a special Author, but its words are just that. They are words that you can read and understand. Most passages can be easily understood by the sincere student who reads them simply and allows the words to speak for themselves.

Interpret the Meaning. Once you have observed what the text *says,* try to understand what the passage meant and *means.* Your personal Bible study should move you from capturing the content of the passage to grasping its concepts. Interpretation is much like observation and often will happen at the same time. Interpreting takes observation one step further, however, by "translating" the text into your own words, thoughts, and level of understanding.

Anytime communication takes place between two parties, there is potential for misunderstanding. We may hear and understand perfectly what someone *says,* but still wonder what they *mean.* Interpreting the meaning of the passage is where we seek to clarify the author's intent.

Always consider the passage's context. Never read or study a passage in isolation. Try to discover or determine what was happening before and after the passage as well as the writer's and readers' historical context.

Compare the passage to other passages in the Bible. The Bible is its own best commentary. It never contradicts itself when interpreted correctly. By comparing passages, you can see how the Holy Spirit led other biblical writers to speak to the same issue or issues.

Read other resources such as commentaries, Bible handbooks, and Bible dictionaries. God's people have always written about the Bible. Through the centuries the church has acquired an enormous amount of information that can help you understand the text. Keep in mind that while God's Word is inerrant, the commentaries are not. Don't limit yourself to just one writer or source.

Write down what you consider to be the timeless truth or truths of the passage. Can this truth be applied in any time and any place, with any people? Observing the text will reveal what the text says with all of its original cultural and historical setting. Interpretation attempts to strip away the cultural setting to reveal the eternal truth of the passage.

Apply the Truth. Personal Bible study must go beyond observation and interpretation to application. In applying the truth, do several things.

First, understand what the truth means in your own personal context. What does it mean to *you?* How is the truth relevant to you as parent, employee, adult, or leader. Is your context anything like the context of the first readers?

Second, ask what kind of conflict the truth is creating in your thinking and life.

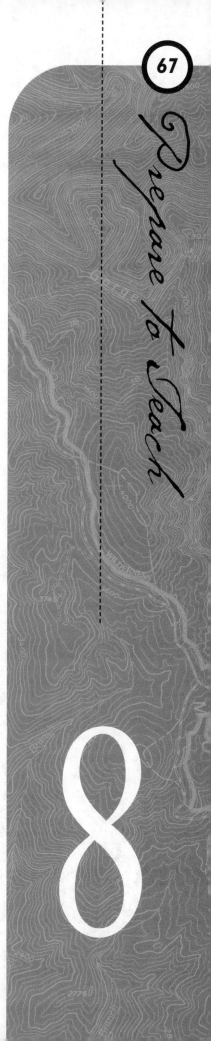

How do you need to change? Is there a gap between what you really believe and what the Bible says and means? Adults most often learn best when some kind of life conflict is created. Teachers should always seek to identify if personal conflict is created through personal study of the Bible.

Third, ask God to plant the truth deep in your heart so that it becomes a personal conviction. This may happen immediately or may takes weeks or months. It is here that God's truth becomes *your* truth. It is, of course, truth whether you believe it or not. Once it becomes a conviction, however, it is in a position to bring about spiritual transformation in your own life.

Fourth, identify how the truth will change your conduct. How should your life change as a result of your new conviction? Sometimes our patterns of behavior become so fixed that we do things without thinking. Personal Bible study should be deliberate in considering the implications of the truths we discover.

You are more than a pipeline through which lessons flow. You must encounter the Scripture yourself and experience the tension between where you are and where God wants you to be. Personal Bible study should accomplish this in your life. Pray and ask God to transform you by His Spirit and the truth of His Word. God is already at work in your life and the lives of your learners. Your preparation needs to acknowledge His activity and your dependence on His power.

The Leader is the Lesson

Teachers who teach for spiritual transformation not only teach a lesson, they *are* the lesson. Transformationl Bible teaching requires you to model the truth that God indeed does transforms lives. In his letter to Timothy, Paul wrote: "Don't let anyone look down on you because you are young, but *set an example for the believers in speech, in life, in love, in faith and in purity* (2 Tim. 4:12; italics added).

Jesus provided an example of how we teach to impact the lives of learners. Whether communicating an eternal truth to His disciples (Matt. 16:13-19) or having dinner with tax collectors (Luke 15:1-2; 19:1-27), He was always teaching and always *being* the lesson. You teach by your example. Your life first must become a living example of the lesson and Bible truth as you live with and before others in life's normal routines.

As you prepare for the session, keep this mind. The life you live before learners will say more than your words or learning activities. If personal Bible study and preparation doesn't lead you to become an example of the truth you're teaching, then something is terribly wrong. This doesn't mean you must be perfect or even have the truth fully integrated into your own convictions. It does mean, however, that there is more to teaching than dispensing information or even truth. The leader is the lesson. You need to encounter God's Word and be transformed by it before you lead your learners to encounter it.

Alan Raughton is Manager, Adult Ministry Services Section, Sunday School Group, LifeWay Church Resources, and teaches a coed Bible study group for young adults at New Hope Baptist Church, Hermitage, TN.

[1]Additional information regarding elements of Sunday School leadship meetings can be obtained from *Adult Sunday School for a New Century,* by Richard E. Dodge and Rick Edwards.

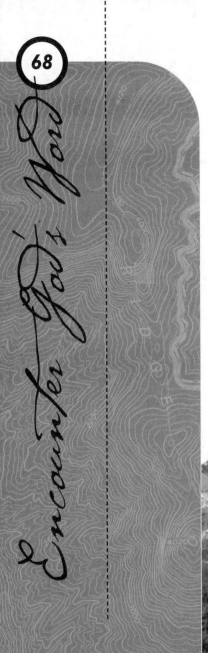

Encounter God's Word

9

by Terry
Hadaway

Before selecting a path, hikers first must determine where they will begin and end their hike. Typically, the focus of the journey is not the path; the path simply guides people to their destinations. Yes, the paths are important. Paths may provide sure footing or safe passageways so hikers can discover what lies along the paths. But the paths are the means to the ends.

Solid Bible teaching is a path that moves people from one spiritual point to another. A well-conceived Bible study session should be a path that connects us to God through His Word. The journey can be very exciting because meaningful Bible study can take adults to places where they have never been. Sometimes the journey may be rigorous and challenging for leader and learner alike. At other times the journey will guide travelers peacefully through gentle reminders of God's love and grace. The prepared direction given by a careful guide can take adults to places that can transform every part of their lives.

The journey through God's Word is an exciting and transforming adventure. Guiding learners through God's Word also is an awesome responsibility. God deserves the best efforts every leader can give. The path leaders take from the beginning of the session to the time learners walk out the classroom door should lead participants to experience the transforming power of the God. The mature leader will understand the need to prepare, study, and work at being the best guide possible, "a workman who does not need to be ashamed and who correctly handles the word of truth."

Encountering God's Word

In the last chapter we considered what it means to Prepare before the session. In this chapter we will think about the Encounter with God's Word that takes place during the session. There are many parts in a typical Bible study session, such as prayer, fellowship, and announcements. However, an encounter with the living and powerful Word of God is still the main reason for gathering.

Bible study is not an optional part of the session, it *is* the session. Because of the importance of God's Word, we must lift up and teach with intense commitment to Bible study. Paul emphasized this to Timothy: "All Scripture is God-breathed and is useful for teaching, rebuking, correcting and training in righteousness, so that the man of God may be thoroughly equipped for every good work (2 Tim. 3:16-17).

Spiritual transformation in the lives of adults cannot take place apart from an encounter with the Bible. The Bible is the truth that transforms. Paul described God's work of spiritual transformation as "the renewing of your mind" (Rom. 12:2). Peter declared, "For you have been born again, not of perishable seed, but of imperishable, through the living and enduring word of God" (1 Pet. 1:23).

Encounter God's Word

9

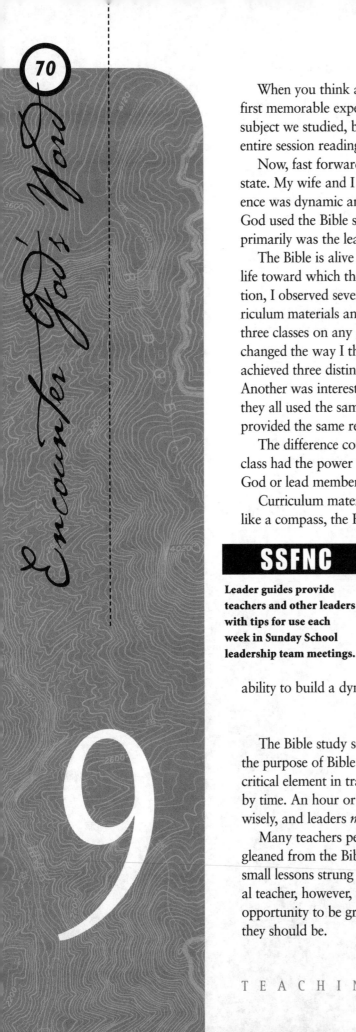

Encounter God's Word

9

The Leader Makes the Difference

When you think about the typical Bible study group, what comes to mind? My first memorable experience in such a group was as a teenager. I cannot recall the subject we studied, but I do remember one thing: It was boring! The leader spent the entire session reading aloud every word in the teacher's book.

Now, fast forward several years with me. Years later I am in a church in another state. My wife and I are part of a Bible study group for young adults. This experience was dynamic and exciting. We learned a great deal about God and His Word. God used the Bible study to change us. The difference between the two experiences primarily was the leader!

The Bible is alive and life-changing. Bible study experiences should reflect the life toward which the Bible guides us. While doing research for my doctoral dissertation, I observed several Sunday School classes. Each class was using the same curriculum materials and, because of multiple Sunday School hours, I was able to visit three classes on any given Sunday. One week, I witnessed a series of events that changed the way I think about teaching the Bible. I experienced three leaders who achieved three distinctly different results. One class was dynamic and exciting. Another was interesting, but not captivating. The third class simply was boring. Yet, they all used the same curriculum materials, taught the same age group, and were provided the same resources.

The difference could be summed up in two words: the teacher. The leader of each class had the power to guide learners toward a transformational encounter with God or lead members toward an early nap.

Curriculum materials are resources teachers can use to guide a journey. Much like a compass, the Bible study resources merely take us in a direction. Good teaching can overcome weaknesses in curriculum materials, but great materials cannot overcome weak teaching. It's you, the leader, that really makes the difference.

SSFNC

Leader guides provide teachers and other leaders with tips for use each week in Sunday School leadership team meetings.

There is a difference between being a teacher and being a great teacher—a transformational teacher. Too often, great teachers are few and far between. What makes a teacher great? Any number of characteristics could be listed.

Certainly one of the most important characteristics is the ability to build a dynamic, purposeful plan for leading the Bible study session.

Viewing the Session Holistically

The Bible study session is that period of time when the group actually meets for the purpose of Bible study. How the Bible teacher leads the session is obviously a critical element in transformational teaching. Most Bible study sessions are limited by time. An hour or less is typical for most Bible study sessions. Time *must* be used wisely, and leaders *must* view each session holistically.

Many teachers perceive the session merely as a period of time to fill with lessons gleaned from the Bible. For these teachers, the session is little more than a series of small lessons strung together, ending with the bell and a prayer. The transformational teacher, however, understands that the session is not a time slot to be filled, but an opportunity to be grasped in order to move learners from where they are to where they should be.

The difference in these two perspectives is profound. The first perspective is leader-centered, driven by content and merely seeking to deliver as much content as possible in the time allotted. The second perspective is transformational and learner-centered. It is driven by a purpose and seeks to change—or at least challenge—how learners think. The first perspective is fragmented, the second is holistic.

Transformational Bible teachers view each session as a single opportunity to achieve a single purpose in learners' lives. They understand where learners are in their understanding of God and His Word, and where the learners should be. They will then build a session plan for moving learners toward the desired goal.

Begin With the End in Mind

A young man rushed home and informed his wife that they were taking a vacation. The excitement in his voice grew as he talked about the fun and relaxation they would experience. He rushed to the bedroom and began packing. His wife watched in amazement. She, too, was happy about the opportunity for a vacation, but she had several questions. Finally, she got her husband's attention and said, "It's great that we're going on a vacation, but where are we going?"

The young man stopped tossing clothes into his luggage, looked, and said, "I knew I forgot something!" In his excitement, he had forgotten to select a destination. How ridiculous it would be to begin a vacation without a clue as to where your are going.

Session after session, Bible teachers prepare to take their classes on a journey. However, many teachers enter class without a clearly defined goal for each session. Teachers need to prepare for each session first by identifying where they want to go with the lesson. Teachers are guides for a Bible study *journey*. The spiritual lives of members in many ways are in a teacher's hands. Where will the teacher be taking the group today? What does the teacher want to accomplish? Where does the teacher want learners to be at the close of the session?

Start with the Learners

The place to start in developing a session goal is with learners themselves. How well do you know the spiritual conditions of your learners? If learners are typical, their spiritual depth will vary. One challenge facing adult Bible teachers is discerning learners' spiritual starting points. The good news is that teachers can know something about the spiritual conditions of learners. Doing so, however, takes time.

A learner's spiritual condition often can be discovered rather easily through personal interaction. Many leaders invest time visiting learners in their homes or on the phone. As leaders talk and interact with learners, they can guide the discussion toward spiritual matters by asking questions about the learner's spiritual background and that of family members. Ask about church involvement, leadership positions held now or in the past, and so forth. In a single conversation, leaders can determine if the learner is saved or lost and the degree to which a learner's faith influences other areas of life. This information helps leaders know where to begin when discussing spiritual matters.

Encounter God's Word

9

Determine the Biblical Truth

Each session should seek to move learners toward a better understanding of God and His kingdom. Each session should focus on a primary biblical truth that grows out of the Bible text to be studied. The teacher should ask, "If I can communicate only *one* Bible truth during this session, what will it be?" Many truths could be examined in any single session, but teachers should have one *primary* biblical truth in mind and direct the session from that one truth. For example, in a Bible study on 1 John 4:7-21, the biblical truth might be: God is a loving God, and He expects believers to show His love through their lives and words. Other relevant truths could be discovered in this passage. Teachers must determine, however, which truth will be the primary biblical truth to be addressed during the session.

Consider the Life Impact

It's not enough merely to communicate one or more biblical truths. Teachers should seek to impact each learner's life in some specific way in each session. Teachers should ask, What difference do I want this session to make in the lives of my learners? As with the biblical truth, there may be many possible ways the session could impact someone's life. Still, teachers should have in mind some specific difference the session should make in the learners. Using 1 John 4:7-21 again, a good life impact statement might be: To help you show God's love through your life and words. This statement reflects the biblical truth while indicating the desired impact on the learner. These two elements—the biblical truth and the desired life impact— will form an appropriate, learner-centered goal for the session. Now the question becomes, How will teachers move learners toward this goal?

SSFNC

Word studies in learner guides can be used by teachers to add depth to group discussions.

The Seven Elements of Transformational Learning

Once a goal has been established for the session, transformational teachers will begin building session plans designed to move learners from where they are toward a better understanding of the biblical truth and toward a lifestyle that reflects that truth. This plan should take into account seven essential elements of transformational learning. These seven elements provide a general representation of how transformational learning takes place. They do not represent a fixed process by which each step is clearly distinct from the others. Neither is the list intended to be a teaching plan itself. These elements can, however, help teachers understand what needs to happen in learners' lives as they encounter the Word of God. At some point in the transformational learning process, learners should:

Acknowledge Authority. Every learner comes to the session with some authority—some power, assumption, presupposition, or rule—that **controls** his or her life. Who or what is the authority that is in control of my life? Teachers need to lead learners to acknowledge this authority so learners will recognize that the question is not *whether* something will control them, but *who* or *what* will control them.

This element sets the stage for transformational learning. It's here that learners begin to see that their perspective shapes the way they live. When they acknowledge an authority in their lives, they are acknowledging that they are driven by some worldview or faith system. They are acknowledging that they are not merely machines. They think, they believe, and they act on the basis of their beliefs. They also are acknowledging that they can change the way they think and believe. They can learn and live in a new way. They are making themselves vulnerable to change.

How teachers lead learners to acknowledge authority will vary. Change may not be overt and noticeable in every session. Teachers must recognize, however, the value of this phase in the learning process and seek to incorporate it into the session. To help you remember this element, note the word *control.*

Search the Truth. If a group is going to study the Bible, then learners must at some point open and examine the **content** of the actual Bible text. What historical setting and key words are reflected in the content of this Bible text? To answer this, learners need to know the intended meaning of specific words and phrases. Literary factors (poetry, sermonic, and so forth), historical factors (customs, geography, events, and so forth), and the broader context of Scripture should be considered.

This is an essential element in transformational learning and should be present in every session. Here learners encounter the objective Word of God as an external reality. Learners discover that God has spoken. They may not like what God says, but they can't dismiss it as though it's not there. In time, this alone will have an impact on the learner's worldview. Searching the Scriptures consistently reinforces the truth that God is personal and He speaks objectively. The key word here is *content.*

Discover the Truth. It is not enough to explore only what the Bible content actually says. Teachers and learners need to ask, So what? What eternal concept is the Holy Spirit revealing to me from this Scripture? This **concept** should be applicable for anyone, anytime, anywhere. What does God want to communicate through this text to people living today? What abiding biblical truth is the Holy Spirit teaching about thinking, feeling, and living today?

This element also is essential to every session. This is the point at which it becomes clear that the Bible is not a dead book with no relevance to people today. Here learners are exposed to the idea that truth is absolute and timeless. What was true for people in the Bible is true for people today. In planning for the session, this is where teachers should articulate the biblical truth to be conveyed.

In most instances, this is where the session moves from examination of biblical content to examination of a relevant concept. This doesn't mean, however, that content always precedes concept. A teacher may choose to introduce the biblical truth (concept) *before* the group actually looks at the Bible text (content). How this is done is up to the teacher and points to the need for the teacher to be intentional in planning for the session. The key word for this element is *concept.*

Personalize the Truth. During the session, learners need to take the universal truth or concept and begin to make personal application to their own lives. Sooner or later learners need to personalize the truth by bringing it into their own particular world or **context.** In my life context, what is God teaching me personally from this Scripture? The teacher should consider generational, developmental, and life-stage factors in helping learners personalize the truth. This element should occur fairly naturally as the group studies the Bible text and sees ways the text applies to them.

Personalizing the truth (context) is another element that should be present in every session. While they do not always have to occur in this order, content, concept, and context are essentials that teachers can control. These are the only por-

Encounter God's Word

tions of the lesson that teachers can accomplish with some certainty. That's why teachers should build these into every session. *Context* is the word to remember with this element.

Struggle with the Truth. None of us is perfect. When confronted with God's truth (concept) in a personal way (context), every adult will experience a degree of **conflict** as he or she sees the gap between what God desires and the way things really are in our lives. The Holy Spirit can use this conflict to bring about a sense of remorse and a desire to change. What conflict or crisis of belief is the Holy Spirit bringing about in my heart and life? What life questions, problems, issues, or struggles compel you to seek answers and promises in the Bible? This internal, spiritual struggle is essential to transformational teaching and learning. It is where the learner begins to see the need for a different perspective and way of thinking.

Struggling with the truth may be the single most important essential in transformational learning . . . and probably the most difficult to control. Teachers can communicate the truth of God's Word in personal and relevant ways, but how individual learners receive the truth depends on the learner and the Holy Spirit. In most instances, the struggle may begin during the session, but will take place primarily beyond the session. This is where leaders must depend on prayer and God's power to bring about conflict in a learner's life. Even though it is impossible to make it happen, the teacher should always plan for conflict to occur. The key word to remember here is *conflict*.

Believe the Truth. As learners struggle with the truth, they naturally will deal with certain questions: What new biblical conviction is God leading me to integrate into my life? How is the Holy Spirit leading me to repent or to change my mind, my values, or the way I live? Conflict is hard to live with, so your learners will seek to resolve the struggle one way or another. They may choose to reject the truth and continue believing as they have. On the other hand, they may accept the truth as valid and choose to believe it as a matter of personal **conviction.** You cannot program how or when this will occur. Personal conviction may develop during the session or may occur several weeks or months later. You probably will not know by the end of the session whether anyone has deepened or developed a conviction.

Believing the truth is a critical point in the transformational process because a person's convictions become the basis for his or her behavior. It's one thing for an individual to acknowledge the authority of God's Word and relevance of a biblical truth. It's another for the learner to adopt the truth as a part of his or her own worldview. It's also important to recognize the difference between profession and conviction. Many people will profess that certain truths are part of their personal belief system (their worldview). That does not mean, however, that those truths have reached a level of personal conviction and are now guiding the person's behavior. Transformation occurs when truth has been integrated into a learner's personal convictions to the point that it now guides his or her behavior. The key word here is *conviction*.

Obey the Truth. Jesus said, "If you love me, you will obey what I command" (John 14:15). In the final analysis, our conduct demonstrates our love for Christ. If

teaching fails to lead the learner to obey the truth of God's Word, then no real transformation has occurred. Transformational teaching needs to guide learners to identify ways they will act on the lesson in obedience. How is the Holy Spirit changing my conduct in how I think, what I value, and the way I live? In some instances, the lesson may actually provide opportunity for obedience during the encounter itself. In other instances, obedience will not be possible until after the session.

This element poses the question, To what extent will you love, trust, and obey the Lord in what you think and value and the way you live? This is not a matter of convincing the learner to do something by "twisting their arm" or manipulating them into action. It's a matter of helping the learners discover how God would have them conduct themselves in light of the convictions they have developed through encountering God's Word. *Conduct* is the key word to remember for this element.

The seven elements of control, content, concept, context, conflict, conviction, and conduct are intended to help you understand the general process that occurs in a person's life as he or she encounters God's Word and experiences transformation. These seven elements are not designed to represent steps in a teaching plan. As you plan a session, don't feel the need to create a seven-step plan that reflects all seven elements. More than one of the elements might be addressed in a single, brief step. You may find the need to repeat one or more throughout a session or unit, much like a spiral advances through a series of repeated movements.

Crafting a Strong Teaching Plan

As you identify learning activities to use to guide learners through various phases of transformational learning, think about how to craft an effective, transformational teaching plan. A strong teaching plan will do several things.

- *Strong teaching plans identify how the session needs to end.* Too often the clock, not the teacher, determines how the session ends. Know how to end the session before determining how it will start. Begin with the end in mind!
- *Strong teaching plans have time-segment estimates.* Teachers who fail to do this are much more likely to run of out time in the session and lose the closure that is needed. Don't let a great finish get pushed out because the bell rings. Think about the time needed for each activity.
- *Strong teaching plans grab attention from the beginning.* Do your best to stimulate interest. If you lose your learners, you may never get them back. Select learning activities that will communicate the lesson is relevant and of value.
- *Strong teaching plans call for a variety of teaching methods and learning activities.* Select teaching activities that capture the interest of learners. Teachers who know the learning styles of their members can identify attention-grabbing methods by referring to the chart on pages 94-95. Using methods that match how adults learn helps teachers capture and maintain interest.
- *Strong teaching plans address a variety of learning styles.* Most classes will have several learning styles represented in every session. Using several approaches to teaching will engage a larger number of your learners.
- *Strong teaching plans lead learners through all seven essentials of transformational learning.* Although not all of the essentials will be necessary in every session, a balanced approach based on careful planning assures that all essentials are covered in two or three weeks.

• *Strong teaching plans expose learners to the entire Bible passage.* This can be done in segments or all at once. If done in segments, be careful to pace your time so you don't bog down and run out of time. If done all at once, plan to do so at a time when it can achieve the greatest impact. This can come early or late in the session.

The Scripture Outline

In planning the encounter, consider the Scripture text and how it is divided. The passage may be outlined for you already in some curriculum materials. If not, develop a simple outline that addresses each Bible segment. A good Scripture outline helps capture the flow of the passage and communicate that flow to learners.

Be careful however not to perceive the Scripture outline as a teaching outline. The passage outline can be a helpful tool, but don't let it become the teaching plan. If the Scripture outline and teaching plan are confused, the session can become nothing more than a string of smaller lessons based on the passage segments. This fragments the session and tends to exclude certain key elements of transformational learning.

Each session needs to focus on one primary biblical truth that leads to one primary life impact. Teachers who merely move learners through a Scripture outline probably will cover several biblical truths and several life impact goals in a single session. Each truth then loses the impact it might have had.

Learner Guides

Transformational Bible study will engage each learner at two distinct times: *during* the session and *beyond* the session. Effective Bible teachers will work to accomplish this through strong teaching plans and strong relationships. Learner resources, however, should not be overlooked as an effective tool for engaging learners both in the session and beyond the session. A good Bible study learner guide will do several things:

SSFNC

In selected learner guides, interactive questions and activities are provided that can engage learners in Bible study following the lesson or can be used during the session.

• Help people develop Bible knowledge and Christian convictions based on sound biblical exposition.
• Encourage learners to develop lifelong Bible study skills and Christian disciplines by providing Bible study helps.
• Provide attractive visuals that engage people in reflective questions and biblical insights.
• Challenge readers to make a personal commitment to obey what God is teaching them.
• Support a diversity of learning styles.
• Provide leaders with an economical tool for involving people during the session for Bible research and response.
• Engage people in personal study and reflection beyond the session.

To strengthen the Bible study experience, provide a Bible study guide for each Bible study participant. Use learner guides in the Bible study session as a tool for exploring the Bible passage. Show participants how to use the learner guide as a spiritual growth resource before and/or after the session.

A creative Bible teacher will recognize that the learner guide has tremendous potential as a resource for use during the session. Segments of commentary can be read and discussed. Maps, photos, and illustrations can be used to generate discussion and reflection. Some learner guides build in learning activities designed to be used specifically during the session.

The more a learner is exposed to and encouraged to use the learner guide during the session, the more familiar with the book he or she will become. A dynamic Bible study session that utilizes the learner guide can encourage the learner to use the resource at home either as a follow-up to the lesson or in preparation for the next session. As you build a plan to lead the encounter, look for ways to use this valuable teaching tool.

Leader Resources

Many teachers develop their own teaching plans for leading the encounter with God's Word. Others rely on suggested teaching plans found in some kind of leader guide. A third group will start with suggested teaching plans and adapt them to meet the needs of their particular groups.

There are a number of advantages to using some kind of leader resource as a teacher. Leader resources often reflect the thinking of a group of people who are familiar with Bible study resources. Their experience will find its way into the leader guide, helping you avoid a variety of problems you may encounter if you try to go it alone.

In addition, leader guides typically provide commentary to enhance understanding of the passage and other teaching helps to strengthen your teaching and make the session successful. Posters, hand-outs, and electronic supplements are just some of the sorts of things available to teachers today.

Sometimes leader resources will offer help for the total Bible teaching ministry, recognizing that transformational teaching must take place in the larger ministry environment. While many Bible teachers are quite creative and resourceful, the busy world in which we live makes effective leader resources a wonderful tool for the transformational Bible teacher.

An Exciting Adventure

The journey through adult education is an exciting adventure. Leading adults indeed is a privilege and an awesome responsibility. As you lead adults in an encounter with the Bible, you will find the path to spiritual growth beneficial for both your learners and yourself. As you grow, you will find learners growing. It's contagious!

Terry Hadaway is Editor of Young Adult and Collegiate Bible study resources, Adult Biblical Studies Section, LifeWay Church Resources, Nashville, TN., and teaches an adult Bible study group at First Baptist Church, Hendersonville, TN.

SSFNC

In addition to leader and learner guides, transformational teachers can find extended interpretive information about biblical history, words, characters, cities, and more in *Biblical Illustrator.* **Teachers also can find illustrations and information for each lesson written within two weeks prior to the lesson by logging onto the Adult Sunday School website at www.lifeway.com/biblein-sites. Look for** *EXTRA!* **suggestions.**

10

by Alan
Raughton

My son Ben and I raced down the Rio Grande River in New Mexico one summer with a group of friends who went white-water rafting. Yellow Bird, a competent guide who knew just where to aim the raft, directed us easily through passes and channels that were safe and fun. Had we been rafting without a capable guide, we could have been injured if the raft had slammed into large boulders along the edge or hidden beneath the flow.

Competent guides are necessary for navigating many of the paths we follow. Trained guides lead tour groups through national forests and parks. Guides may take us through a museum or art gallery. Sometimes we might enlist a guide to take us through unfamiliar parts of a major city, or we may join a tour group that will travel through several foreign countries.

Competent guides are necessary for leading us through some of the difficult paths that life may take as well. Not all paths are clear and marked. We often say that a young adult who has been arrested has wandered off the right paths or is following the wrong one. Can we find guides today who will lead us along the right paths and help us cope with crises that could lead us off the right paths?

The Paths of Life

Most of us would agree that the Bible acts as a compass through the paths of life. If we follow the direction set out in Scripture, we will be pointed along the right paths through life. But even dedicated Christians who generally try to head toward true north in life may wander off the paths. Christians still wrestle with the struggles of life that can lead them along paths that can destroy life: questionable business transactions, sexual temptations, and such. Teaching the Bible is more than completing a lesson plan during the appointed time in the session. A competent guide for life today is someone who seeks opportunities for ministry and spiritual growth with learners and with those who have not yet discovered the real path, the path of faith in Christ.

A guide has been defined as one who directs a person in his conduct or course of life. Adult Bible teachers must wrestle with this definition as they consider how they relate to their learners. The "paths of life" will take your learners, and you, far beyond the session. As leaders called by God to lead a group of adults toward spiritual growth, the role of teacher cannot be taken lightly. Spiritual transformation, of course, is God's work of changing a believer. However, competent Bible study guides can facilitate the work of the Holy Spirit in their own lives and in the lives of their learners.

A national park guide may be quite familiar with the park, but still takes people along paths where the followers are fascinated by the sights, sounds, and experiences along the path. The elements of a lesson can be markers along a pathway that move adults from where they are now to where God wants them to be. Your spiritual *preparation* before the session connects with an *encounter* with the Word during the session in the context of your Bible study group. Together, you try to steer the course of the lesson along well-marked trails that lead to personal discovery, but the trip does not end with the close of the session.

Continuing the Lesson

Teaching does not stop when the session is over. Teachers continue their teaching ministry regardless of time, place, or situation. Teachers—in fact, all leaders—become examples of the Christ-like life. How? By spending time daily with the Lord, praying for Bible study group learners and families by name, and by working through other group leaders who in turn connect with others in the group. Ministry leaders, for example, can become extensions of the teacher's work by calling or visiting ministry team members to talk about the lesson. Teachers become guides when they stay in touch with members and prospects, build fellowship, and engage in ministry.

SSFNC

New suggestions are included each week in leader and learner guides to help adults continue the lesson after the session.

The long-term value of relationships is seen in the lives of Paul and Timothy. Nearing death, Paul reminded his understudy that Timothy learned the Scriptures relationally, first from his mother and grandmother (2 Tim. 1:5) and then from

10

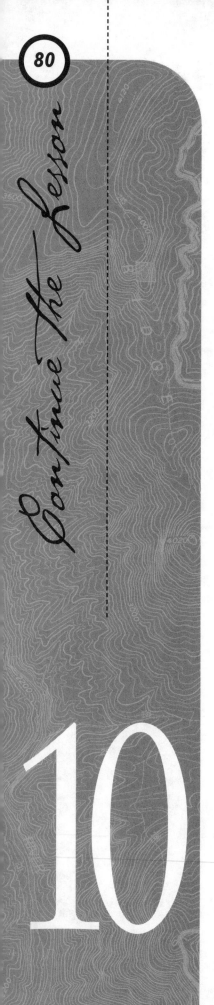

others whom he knew (2 Tim. 3:14). Timothy was to follow this pattern of instruction with faithful men who in turn could teach others (2 Tim. 2:2).

God can use every teacher's ministry beyond the classroom to continue the lesson he or she started in the session. People desperately want to make sense of what is happening with God, their friends, their families, their churches, their careers, and their world. The transformational Bible teacher can help learners struggle with the truth of God's Word and move toward spiritual transformation by continuing the lesson *after* the session.

Bible Study and The Family

Adults will sense a greater responsibility to continue the lesson in their personal lives when they are reminded of the impact the lesson can have on their children or other family members. Bible study groups can partner with parents, affirming the home as the center of biblical guidance. In addition, they can help train Christian parents, including single parents, to fulfill their responsibilities as the primary Bible teachers and disciplers of their children.

SSFNC

Both the Explore the Bible Series and the Family Bible Study Series provide support for a weekly family Bible study experience. An icon or label will identify this element in both the leader and learner guides.

God used the biblical prophets to lead, discipline, challenge, and comfort. He used them to teach. But the prophets never operated within a spiritual vacuum. Their messages were delivered within the context of a community of faith, a spiritual body. Within that community there were smaller units called families that God ordained to be the primary unit for teaching the faith. That is still true today.

The Bible consistently affirms the family's strategic role in the kingdom of God. In the family, God establishes our most significant relationships and builds our character. No Bible study group can take the place of the family and its responsibility to be the center of biblical guidance. As much as possible, the transformational Bible teacher needs to partner with the family in this holy endeavor. Here are some suggestions for how to do this.

- Recognize the power of the family in building, or possibly destroying, personal faith.
- Create a bank of information for each family represented in your class. This information gives you valuable insight into your learners' lives.
- Recognize special events or circumstances in each learner's life. Simple things like an anniversary card or a phone call on a child's birthday can strengthen your role and place in the learner's family.
- Meet and get acquainted with other family members. You can learn a lot about a learner by watching children and other family members.
- Inquire about the spiritual condition of family members. Many families have unsaved parents, spouses, or children.
- Encourage family enrichment activities. These can be wonderful opportunities for learners to reflect on truths learned in Bible study.
- Encourage a family Bible study time each week. A brief time once a week when the family gathers to study and discuss God's Word can be a powerful activity with value far beyond that week's lesson.

Engaging Learners After the Session

Recognizing the role of the family is critical to continuing the lesson after the session. There are, however, some other very practical things you can do to engage your learners in the lesson after the session.

Shepherd your flock. Jesus said, "I am the good shepherd; I know my sheep and my sheep know me—just as the Father knows me and I know the Father—and I lay down my life for the sheep." (John 10:14-15) As the spiritual leader of a class, teachers can never impact learners' lives if they don't truly know their learners. Take time to get to know learners outside of class. Teachers can invite them to their homes or go to dinner with them. Encourage learners to discuss their hopes and fears. Ask questions about their current activities and where they stand in their personal spiritual pilgrimages.

Solicit testimonies. Ask people to share with others in their study group how a particular lesson made a difference in their lives. Teachers can plan testimonies into their teaching plans and enlist learners in advance to give testimonies. Preparing for this causes learners to reflect on what they have studied and consider what they might need to do to stay on the right paths. By sharing with the class, they feel a higher degree of accountability to the group. Such sharing allows teachers to discover ways God is working in learners' lives.

Encourage accountability. Effective teachers hold themselves as well as their learners accountable for obeying what the Bible teaches. Learners rightfully expect their teachers to come prepared to teach. What if the learners came prepared to share what God has taught them or how God has used them in ministry since the previous session? Teach adults that they too are guides for others to follow. All Christians must accept the role of guide for the lost because without a guide, they are not likely to discover the path to faith. Learners who testify to how a lesson equipped them to witness, minister, or simply connect personally with a lost person may encourage a reluctant believer to do the same.

Involve Learners in Ministry. Teachers are to guide other class leaders to effective service. Encourage class leaders and learners to work together to minister to people who are hurting or suffering loss. Such opportunities help learners focus on the needs of others and develop a spirit of love and compassion. When adults visit a hospitalized member or prospect, ministry is taking place. When ministry team members contact their assigned members to ask how to pray specifically for them this week, ministry is taking place. Ministry often provides a practical way to apply the lesson.

Involve in Evangelism. Encourage leaders and learners to invite lost friends, neighbors, or work associates with them to the Bible study session. In the impersonal climate of today's world, Bible study experiences in a small group setting can meet important needs of people who have lost a sense of personal identity

Continue the Lesson

and self-worth. Experiencing a human touch, meeting friends, and developing a closeness to God can lead individuals to know the joys and personal relationships available in the body of Christ. When lost people attend the session, enlist someone from the class to visit these individuals at home to share the message of Christ. If your church uses the FAITH Sunday School Evangelism Strategy®, become personally involved in this ministry and encourage others in your class to join a FAITH team.

Pray for your group. Pray daily for your group members and families by name. Praying for them reminds you of their needs and of opportunities to teach through circumstances they are experiencing in their lives. God often uses these times to prompt you to call or write a note at the moment someone needs a special touch from someone. Great encouragement can come through a simple telephone call or note that says, "I am praying for you during this stressful time."

SSFNC

Devotional resources are available for all adults. Devotional elements are included in selected learner guides, while other devotionals are provided through publications such as *Open Windows, Home Life, Stand Firm* (designed for men), *Journey* (designed for women), and *Believe* (designed for new Christians).

Use Email. A simple group message sent to learners during the week takes little time and means a lot. Obtain everyone's email address while getting other personal information, such as home address and telephone number. Email communication among learners is one way teachers can continue the teaching process into the week and encourage learners, too. In fact, encourage learners to discuss the lesson, ask questions of one another, and comment on specific parts of the lesson via email. Many Internet Service Providers (ISP) provide free web page space. Develop a simple web site, and list thoughts about the lesson. A class web page can be a common reference point for learners to visit during the week. The web page may catch the attention of lost people in the community, and can be a place group participants can point friends to for information about a particular lesson or special class activities.

Build fellowship. Your learners will find encouragement and help when they build meaningful relationships with others in the class. Planned fellowship events and a sharing time during the session help accomplish this. As learners' relationships create a sense of community around a personal and common faith, the lesson will continue in the lives of the learners each week.

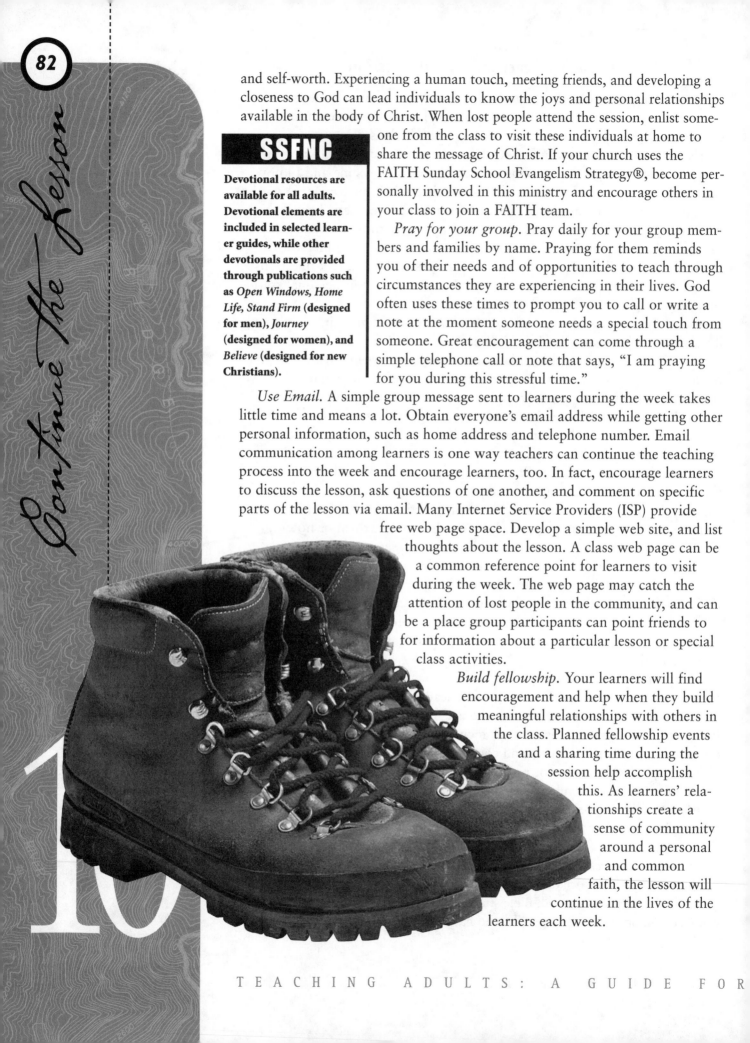

Encourage use of the Bible study Learner Guide during the week. Many Bible study groups use curriculum resources that include learner guides. The learner guide may be designed for use before the session, during the session, after the session, or a combination of these. Regardless of how the materials are designed, encourage learners to review lesson content during the week to support and reinforce the truth studied during the session. Learner guides have great potential in helping your learners continue the lesson.

Encourage a daily devotional time. Each of us needs a daily time of personal prayer and reflection. This should be a time when we focus on God, reflect on His Word, and submit our wills to His. If learners use a devotional resource that relates to the session, the devotional resource becomes a tool to reinforce Bible study. If it doesn't relate to the lesson directly, God still can use the time to speak to learners.

Learning can continue all the time, regardless of the study approach taken. Some of the best learning experiences are spontaneous. Try to continue teaching by helping people connect new truths with what they already know. When people see how God's work in their lives transforms them and they become more like Christ, they will have a framework that the Holy Spirit can use to help them make sense of their day-to-day problems, questions, victories, and joys.

As teachers communicate with learners during the week through conversations, cards, letters, or emails, they can pose questions such as these to explore the lesson further:

- What command did God present?
- What promise did God make?
- What truth did God teach?
- What attitudes, behaviors, or values will you make a part of your life?
- What relationships are you developing in your life that are a part of your journey of becoming a Great Commission Christian?

Thinking Differently

Bible study teachers today must think differently about what constitutes a Bible study lesson. No longer can teachers limit the scope of a lesson to a particular time frame and hope to bring about spiritual transformation in the lives of learners. Teachers must look for ways to continue the lesson beyond the Bible study session. God's work of transforming learners into the image of Christ is a lifelong process. As teachers prepare to teach, they should develop a teaching plan that continues to facilitate the Holy Spirit's ministry for as long as the Lord is working in the lives of learners.

Alan Raughton is Manager, Adult Ministry Services Section, Sunday School Group, LifeWay Church Resources, and teaches a coed Bible study group for young adults at New Hope Baptist Church, Hermitage, TN.

Different Paths to Follow

11

by Joe Sherrer

Family vacations have been fertile storyline sources for movies, comedians, and writers. Indeed, vacations can bring out the dynamic personalities of family members. Family vacations can stimulate wonderful memories, or may ignite terrible family conflict. The very *mention* of a family vacation—cramming family close together in a hotel or the family car—may warm your heart or bring shudders to your soul.

Why does the idea of a family vacation produce such strong emotions? Is it the idea of a required, shared destination? close proximity of family members? the variety of personalities? the way individuals want to approach each task? Could it be varying levels of interest in a chosen activity—or the activities themselves? Perhaps the history of family vacations stimulates positive or negative emotions.

Many of these feelings can be applied to another type of journey: The journey a Bible teacher attempts to lead in a quest for spiritual transformation. In a Bible study, participants are grouped on a shared journey with some type of common aim or goal. Learners bring their common history plus individual backgrounds to the session. Various personalities, learning styles, interests, and needs impact a learner's willingness to "come along for the ride."

During a particular session some learners may want to stop and "visit" a particular "sight" and read all of the information because of a specific need or interest. Other learners may want to pass on through, preferring instead to get to the intended destination: the application of the lesson to real life. Transformational Bible teachers recognize these differences among learners and incorporate strategies in their teaching plans that guide all learners toward spiritual transformation.

Different Paths to Follow

Throughout this chapter we will examine various teaching and learning techniques that help adult teachers conquer these challenges. This chapter will focus on the different paths that can lead adults toward spiritual transformation. We'll explore the different approaches to learning preferred by adults, and teaching methods that engage learners based on these preferences. This chapter also addresses the levels of learning that impact Bible study sessions—understanding how the same session can address different levels of need and understanding. This chapter should encourage you to become a dynamic spiritual guide who can lead adults on a spiritual pilgrimage. So, gear up! We are going to get out our maps and seek paths that can equip teachers to take adult learners on a spiritual quest!

11

Different Paths to Follow

11

Learning Approaches

On one vacation, my family made an unplanned stop at a museum to view an Egyptian art exhibit. One son was delighted. He was ready to examine every artifact, read each brochure, and listen to each museum guide. My other son was not overjoyed, to say it nicely. He grabbed his grandfather in tow, raced through the exhibit in 30 minutes, and proclaimed that he had seen it all and knew it all.

The problem was not simply one of interest or who chose the museum. Not only did the two sons demonstrate different levels of learning, they also approached the learning experience in different ways. One preferred a slow, logical approach; he examined each item, gathered details, and reflected on the significance. My other son's learning approach relates closely to his personality: *charge!* He wanted a rapid overview. If he couldn't touch it, feel it, or in some way experience it, he simply was not interested.

In the same way, adults in a Bible study group vary in their approaches to learning and in their levels of interest and understanding. In a young adult group studying from the Psalms, one participant simply may acknowledge that David wrote the materials. Another may want to experience the beauty and rhythm of the poetry. Still another may enjoy logically linking related verses throughout the Bible to amplify the meaning.

Which adult is approaching Bible study correctly? They all are. Each simply is approaching learning based on an individual learning preference. Most adults can—and do—learn from a variety of learning approaches. They may even have several "favorites." However, learning seems to be maximized when learners are engaged with teaching methods that support their preferred learning approaches.

A variety of systems have been developed to categorize these learning approaches—or preferred learning styles. This chapter will highlight eight approaches through which adults learn: Visual, verbal, natural, logical, musical, reflective, relational, and physical. As you read the brief descriptions of each learning approach think of adults in your Bible study group who prefer to learn using that approach. Write down their names on a piece of paper beside the approach they seem to reflect. Understanding these learning approaches can help you to communicate God's Word more effectively.

• Relational—People who approach learning relationally usually like to be with people. Given a task, they want to do it cooperating and interacting with others. They are often encouragers. Barnabas is a biblical example.

• Musical—Adults who prefer this approach may enjoy singing Scripture verses set to music, writing songs to express spiritual insights, or recording a musical selection for others. Perhaps no better example of a learner who preferred the musical approach exists than David in the Old Testament.

• Logical—Logical learners like step-by-step approaches with each sequence clearly defined. They may be able to analyze new concepts easily, contrasting and comparing aspects to other spiritual truths. The Apostle Paul often presented his doctrinal concepts using logical approaches.

- Natural—Learners who prefer the natural approach like to get into nature. Touching real things, examining the growing process, and determining how to be the best stewards of God's creation appeal to them. Throughout the psalms David formulated many concepts about God through a natural approach.
- Physical—Learners who prefer the physical approach are "hands-on" types. They often have difficulty staying still in class. These adults like to move around, touch things, create manipulative objects, or stand up and act out or dramatize a story. Ezekiel may have been a physical learner as he acted out many of his prophecies.
- Reflective—Pondering situations or mediating on applying God's Word are characteristics of learners who prefer a reflective learning approach. These adults tend to be in touch with who they are and what they feel, and may prefer to work in isolation. Some say Mary is an example of a reflective learner.
- Visual—Visual learners like to "see" the content—either physically see or visualize based on word pictures. Adults who prefer this approach may visualize concepts such as the arrangement of the temple as well as the symbolism implied. John used powerful word pictures in the Book of Revelation.
- Verbal—Adults who prefer the verbal approach like words—whether reading, listening, or writing. These adults like to talk and play word games. Many of the speeches of the Bible—such as ones given by Solomon—are easily related to the verbal learning approach.

Leaders should remember that most adults learn well using multiple approaches to learning—often at the same time or in succession.

Teaching Methods that Support Each Learning Approach

The chart on pages 94-95 identifies teaching methods that can be selected by teachers to appeal to each of the learning approaches. Note that several methods are listed under more than one learning approach. Depending on how these methods are used by teachers or received by learners, these methods can support more than one learning approach.

For example, the question-and-answer method clearly is related to the verbal approach. But this method also may be used in a reflective manner, i.e. "Reflect on the passage we have just studied. How would your life change this week if you were to apply the lesson completely?" Using a role play, where learners act out a situation, may appeal to learners who prefer using the physical approach. The interpersonal dynamics required to prepare the role play also may appeal to learners who enjoy a relational approach.

Selecting teaching methods is closely linked to session aims and goals. For example, an activity that encourages learners to list the sequence of certain biblical events may support a logical approach to learning. However, that activity may not support a teaching aim that is affective in nature—"Learners will develop a deeper appreciation for . . . ." Possible aim or goal "starters" are listed for each of the eight learning approaches. These verbs may suggest possible teaching methods that support both the aim and the learning approach.

SSFNC

Selected leader packs will include CD-ROMs that will provide leaders with digital resources to use in preparation for and presentation during Bible study sessions.

11

Different Paths to Follow

Relational—The chart includes case study, small groups, and storytelling for the relational approach. Consider the following aim and teaching method starters:

- *Learners clarify*—Ask young adults, What does this mean to you?
- *Learners affirm*—Ask senior adults to write a note to a class for young adults encouraging them as new parents.
- *Learners empathize*—Ask learners to tell how they think Mary must have felt when told she was to become a parent.
- *Learners mediate*—Ask learners to role play a conflict and discuss how to resolve the conflict.
- *Learners question*—Ask learners to answer how they would respond to a specific case study.
- *Learners respond*—After viewing a video of media portrayals of contemporary family life, ask young adults to work in small groups to respond to the question, What did not represent Christian family ideals in the video?
- *Learners discuss*—Ask learners to discuss the consequences of behavioral choices that people make.

Musical—Singing is an obvious approach for the musical approach. Writing new words for a common hymn may appeal to musical learners. Teachers who are not confident of their singing abilities can read the words of these creative writing assignments. Starters for this approach may include:

- *Learners listen*—Play a CD of a contemporary Christian song and ask learners to recite a Scripture verse that relates to the song.
- *Learners record*—Ask young adults to write new words to a familiar hymn and record the new song on a cassette to play later for the entire class.
- *Learners sing*—Ask learners to sing a familiar hymn to create interest for a session.
- *Learners compose*—Ask college students to compose a song that expresses the truth of the focal passage.
- *Learners evaluate music*—Play a contemporary song and ask learners to list parts of the song that do not reflect a Christian worldview.
- *Learners play*—Ask learners to clap the rhythm of a hymn or guess the names of hymns as another person hums the tune.
- *Learners adapt or create*—Ask learners to locate a hymn that generally reflects the truth of the lesson and then write an additional verse that encourages them to apply the truth personally.

Logical—Teaching methods that support the logical approach to learning reflect learners' desires for sequentially presented facts and details. Lectures, word studies, and worksheets or study guides appeal to logical learners. Consider these starters for logical learners:

- *Learners organize*—Ask learners to identify the steps necessary to address a specific problem.
- *Learners compare or contrast*—Ask learners to list and then compare how most young adults spend time and money and how the Bible directs Christian stewardship of time and finances.
- *Learners reason*—Ask learners to respond to a series of if/then statements.
- *Learners analyze*—Make a statement about a particular lifestyle and then ask

adults, Why do people act/think/live that way? What will happen to a Christian who continues to act/think/live that way?

- *Learners evaluate*—Show a video or movie clip and ask learners to identify appropriate and inappropriate responses of characters to various situations.
- *Learners rank*—Ask learners to rank in order of importance or value a list of various activities.
- *Learners classify*—Give learners a list of possible activities or programs and ask them to classify them as appropriate for a church to do.

Natural—Learners who prefer the natural approach enjoy interacting directly with items from God's world or related concepts. Teaching methods related to this approach may include activities such as displaying items collected from nature or dealing with such concepts as how Christians can be effective stewards of God's world. While preschoolers might enjoy actually taking a nature walk to observe and collect nature items, adults might take a "mental" nature walk. Consider the following idea starters:

- *Learners dig or touch*—Pass three or four natural objects among learners. Ask them to identify common elements and suggest a truth related to the Scripture passage for the session.
- *Learners observe*—Use an object lesson with learners and ask them to identify a spiritual truth from the illustration.
- *Learners protect*—Ask learners to do a project that reflects Christian stewardship of creation.
- *Learners reflect*—Ask learners to identify principles of science that point to an orderly Creator.
- *Learners collect or display*—Ask a group of adults in advance to collect (or make a list) of items from nature that remind them of a spiritual truth from this week's focal passage.
- *Learners identify*—Ask learners to identify steps of a plan's life cycle as a part of a lesson on spiritual growth.
- *Learners plant or cultivate*—Ask adults to observe growth of a plant as a reminder of their need for spiritual growth through Bible study and prayer.

Physical—The methods chart suggests supporting the physical approach by using an agree/disagree exercise with learners moving to areas of the room to illustrate their opinion. Consider the following idea starters:

- *Learners touch*—Ask learners to join hands in a circle to symbolize unity.
- *Learners recreate*—Ask learners to recreate a model of the temple by using learners as walls and other building features.
- *Learners act or dramatize*—Ask two or three learners to role play a biblical story. Include costumes if possible.
- *Learners move*—Ask adults to move to the appropriate agree/disagree poster, indicating their responses to statements the leader makes.

- *Learners manipulate*—Instruct learners to tear a piece of construction paper into a shape or object representing the most important thing in their lives.
- *Learners play in sports*—Encourage learners to use the church basketball league to exhibit Christ-likeness and open the door to witnessing.
- *Learners display*—Leaders can mail pieces of a puzzle to learners and ask them to bring the pieces the following Sunday. Learners will assemble the puzzle as they come into class to show how parts become the whole and to introduce a session on Christian fellowship.

Reflective—Adults who learn well using the reflective approach usually have good intrapersonal skills. Therefore, asking them to create a personal philosophy about some aspect of the Christian life or to explain their emotions about something may be good ways to involve them in learning experiences. The teaching methods chart suggests several methods that help reflective learners determine, develop, and clarify their personal attitudes or feelings. Some of these include completing open-ended sentences, answering an opinionnaire, or maintaining a diary or journal. The following idea "starters" may suggest other teaching methods that support the reflective approach to learning:

- *Learners meditate*—Encourage learners to think about things for which they are thankful and think about ways God is good to them.
- *Learners evaluate themselves*—Ask learners to identify one weakness in their prayer lives.
- *Learners contemplate*—Ask learners to consider possible results of a particular mistake or potential mistake in their lives.
- *Learners log*—Have learners track the amount of time they spend during the week watching television and in prayer or Bible study.
- *Learners write in journals*—Ask learners to begin a journal of their reflections during personal quiet times. Leaders can share examples of their own journals.
- *Learners personalize*—Ask learners to assume the role of a biblical character in a given situation. Have them identify how they might have responded.
- *Learners ponder*—Ask college students to write a letter to themselves explaining what they think God is directing them to do based on a study session. Leaders can mail the letters to students later as a reminder or encouragement.

Visual—Teaching methods suggested here often allow learners to see something—either actually or conceptually—or create something that allows others to see something are appropriate for adult learners who prefer the visual approach to learning. Teachers can use videos and other media to help learners "see" biblical stories. Using maps or drawing diagrams of biblical events appeal to visual learners. The chart includes a number of methods appropriate for visual learners. Consider the following idea starters:

- *Learners create a mobile or other art object*—Ask learners to create a mini-poster and deliver it to a prospect to invite them to join the group.
- *Learners observe*—Ask learners to complete a worksheet following the viewing of a short video segment that dramatizes a Scripture passage.

- *Learners diagram*—Ask learners to sketch what they think the temple might have looked like based on the Bible's description of the temple.
- *Learners draw or illustrate*—Have learners make a graffiti poster of how the fruit of the Spirit could transform the lives of Christians.
- *Learners demonstrate*—Asks groups of learners to make pictures of one specific part of the armor of Christ and then show that piece to the entire class and assemble the complete armor.
- *Learners paint or view a painting*—Show the familiar picture of Christ standing at a door and knocking. Ask learners to visualize experiences in their lives when they felt Christ knocking at the door of their lives.
- *Learners storyboard*—Asks adults (individually or in groups) to draw a picture of one scene in the story of the Good Samaritan (or any such story being studied). Tape the pictures together in storyboard fashion and show them to the class while the Scripture is reread.

Verbal—Without a doubt, teaching methods supporting the verbal learning approach are among the most common used in Bible study groups. Lectures, case studies, questions and answers, and brainstorming long have been standard tools for Bible study leaders. The chart lists other verbal methods that can strengthen the learning experience for participants who prefer the verbal approach. Listening teams, creative writing, debate, interview, and writing headlines or news stories add creativity to the learning experience. Consider the following idea starters:

- *Learners listen*—Form two listening teams. Each team listens to the same Scripture passage or story, but learners listen from their assigned perspective.
- *Learners paraphrase*—Ask learners to rewrite and then explain the parable of the lost coins into a modern-day version in story format.
- *Learners list*—Ask participants to identify characters in a Bible study and describe how their personalities are like people learners know today.
- *Learners write ideas*—Ask learners to write an article from the perspectives of a soldier and a bystander at Jesus' crucifixion.
- *Learners use humor or stories*—Ask learners to think of humorous or silly phrases we use today that parallel Jesus' example of the plank and speck of dust in a person's eye.
- *Learners report*—Distribute Bible dictionaries and handbooks to the class and asks learners to work in small groups to prepare short reports on the meaning of *grace* and *justification*.
- *Learners label*—Give a list of famous quotations. Ask learners to identify quotations that reflect a biblical worldview and those that do not.
- *Learners recite*—Assign two learners a psalm or other passage to present to the class as a dramatic or responsive reading.

Select Appropriate Methods for Transformation

Remember that the point of using these methods is to get the Bible truth into the lives of learners in such a way that transformation can occur. Although creativity is good, the goal is not to be creative, cute, or see how many methods you can use in one session. Careful attention must be given to using methods that support all learning approaches reflected by learners. Quite simply, this may require

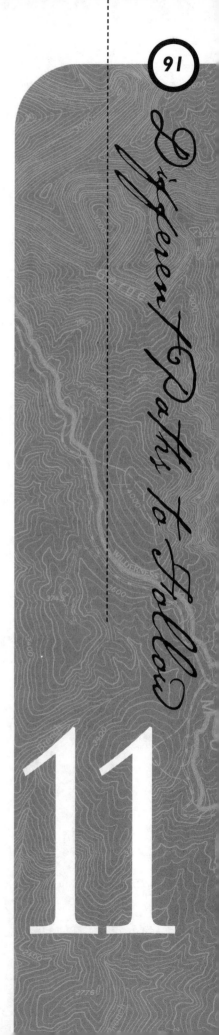

Different Paths to Follow

11

some adjustments from the teacher and learners—both can get stuck in a rut. Ask yourself: Are the needs and interests of all learners being addressed? How could all learners be "stretched" to produce more change in their spiritual lives.

Adult teachers often say, "My class will not do groups!" This complaint indicates the problems many leaders will face when they begin to use teaching methods that support all eight learning approaches. One adult educator suggests helping learners adjust to these changes by making the teaching activity an irresistible invitation to learn. He recommends five criteria for making activities irresistible:

Safe—the adults must feel that their participation will not result in any personal embarrassment from lack of knowledge, personal self-disclosure, or a negative social environment.

Successful—the learners should feel that their efforts will likely be successful and effective.

Interesting—The learning activity should have some parts that are novel, engaging, challenging, or stimulating.

Self-determined—The learners need to be able to make choices that significantly affect the learning experience for themselves. These choices can be made related to what the learners want to share, when or where they will learn, or with whom they will work. The learners will base these choices on their values, needs, concerns, or feelings.

Personally relevant—The leader of an adult group must help the learners to see how their concerns, interests, or prior experiences have been incorporated into the activity to be relevant to their needs.[1]

When these criteria for introducing learning activities are followed, the opportunity for success greatly increases.

> **SSFNC**
>
> **Additional help for selecting appropriate teaching approaches, methods, and resources are available in the Ministry Resources section of leader guides and on the Adult Sunday School website at www.lifeway.com/bibleinsites.**

Levels of Learning

Remember the example of my family at the museum? Both sons were interested—but at obviously different levels of interest. Regardless of the Scripture used in a lesson, learners will respond at different levels of learning. Some educators have used Bloom's approach to levels of learning that specify six levels in the cognitive domain, or areas of knowledge and understanding. The six levels are: knowledge, comprehension, application, analysis, synthesis, and evaluation. A similar system for the affective domain of learning that refers to attitudes and values includes five levels: receiving, responding, valuing, organizing, and characterizing. An excellent application for Christian education for both domains of learning with the various levels has been presented in William Yount's book, *Created to Learn.*[2]

Bible study leaders could consider a somewhat simpler approach to levels of learning. In the following approach, Bible teachers are encouraged to attempt to move learners through the various levels over a period of time. These levels of learning include:

- Exposure
- Recall
- Recognition
- Application
- Lifestyle

An adult teacher using this approach to levels of learning for a study of the concept of forgiveness might incorporate the following items:

- At the exposure level, a learner might hear the concept of forgiveness for the first time and read the Scripture where Jesus says we are to forgive "seventy times seven."
- At the recall level, the learner remembers the concept and the admonition after leaving the Bible study session.
- At the recognition level, the learner would remember the concept so that when offended by someone, the learner might consider this as an opportunity to forgive the offender.
- At the application level, the learner would forgive the offender.
- At the lifestyle level, the learner makes consistent application—consciously and subconsciously—of the concept of forgiveness.

Adult leaders who teach for transformation must remember that they are teaching for the "long haul." Learners at all levels of understanding, a variety of learning approaches, and a multitude of needs and interests inhabit their classes. What an exciting challenge! Enjoy the spiritual pilgrimage! Have a great journey!

[1]Wlodkowski, R. J. *Enhancing Adult Motivation To Learn: A Comprehensive Guide for Teaching All Adults* (2nd edition). San Francisco: Jossey-Bass, 1999.
[2]Yount, William R. *Created to Learn: A Christian Teacher's Introduction to Educational Psychology.* Nashville: Broadman and Holman, 1996, 141-144.

For Further Reading:
Adult Bible study leaders interested in selecting teaching methods that maximize the learning impact may want to consult the following books:
Enhancing Adult Motivation to Learn (2nd edition) by Raymond J. Wlodkowski.
   San Francisco: Jossey-Bass, 1999.
Adults as Learners: Increasing Participation and Facilitating Learning by K. Patricia Cross. San Francisco: Jossey-Bass, 1981.
Called To Teach: An Introduction to the Ministry of Teaching by William R. Yount. Nashville: Broadman and Holman, 1999.
Created to Learn: A Christian Teacher's Introduction to Educational Psychology by William R. Yount. Nashville: Broadman and Holman, 1996.
Planning Programs for Adult Learners: A Practical Guide for Educators, Trainers, and Staff Developers by Rosemary S. Caffarella. San Francisco: Jossey-Bass, 1994.
Learning in Adulthood: A Comprehensive Guide (2nd edition) by Sharan B. Merriam and Rosemary S. Caffarella. San Francisco: Jossey-Bass, 1999.

Joe Sherrer is Professor of Adult Education at New Orleans Baptist Theological Seminary, moving to New Orleans as this book was being completed. Previously he was minister of education, Southern Hills Baptist Church, Oklahoma City, OK.

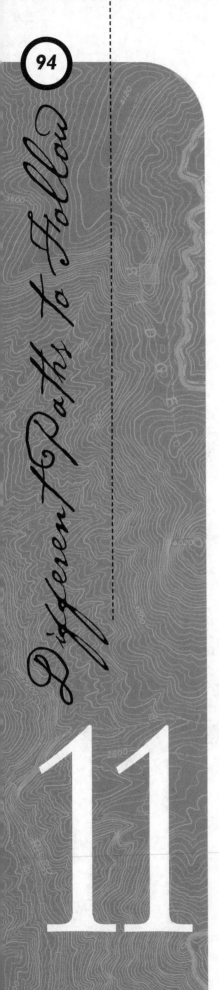

CHOOSING THE

Physical

❑ Move to the appropriate agree/disagree poster indicating their opinions and similar physical actions
❑ Join hands in a circle
❑ Engage in art activities such as wire or paper sculptor, paper tearing, painting, drawing, writing graffiti
❑ Arrange the room for various activities
❑ Games
❑ Sing with motions
❑ Do Biblical simulations
❑ Role play
❑ Skit

Natural

❑ Collect or display items from nature
❑ Conduct a nature walk
❑ Sort items from nature
❑ Classify items from nature
❑ Observe items from nature
❑ Discuss protection of God's world
❑ Reflect on creation and the Creator
❑ Plant, cultivate

Musical

❑ Creative writing (for example, words for well-known hymns)
❑ Recordings, cassette tapes
❑ Singing
❑ Music forum
❑ Finding hymns that reflect the focus of the lesson
❑ Comparing words of hymns to Scripture

❑ Listening to recorded music (sacred or secular) with an assignment in mind
❑ Live musical presentations

Visual

❑ Videos, movie clips, CD ROMs
❑ Posters
❑ Charts
❑ Maps
❑ Paintings
❑ Object lessons
❑ Collage
❑ Wire or paper sculpture
❑ Graffiti
❑ Watching drama
❑ Art activities
❑ Visualizing
❑ Questions that ask "What if . . ."
❑ Drawing diagrams

Relational

❑ Case study
❑ Small groups
❑ Personal sharing/testimony
❑ Storytelling
❑ Circular response
❑ Debate
❑ Interview
❑ Discussion
❑ Panel
❑ Symposium
❑ Biblical simulation
❑ Dialog
❑ Role play
❑ Question and answer
❑ Skit

RIGHT METHODS

- ❏ Games
- ❏ Brainstorming
- ❏ Videos, movie clips
- ❏ Illustrations
- ❏ Problem solving that depends on working with others

Logical

- ❏ Lecture
- ❏ Written test
- ❏ Worksheets and study guides
- ❏ Notebook
- ❏ Outline
- ❏ Word study
- ❏ Statistics
- ❏ Debate
- ❏ Panel
- ❏ Inductive questions
- ❏ Questions that help discern relationships

Verbal

- ❏ Lecture
- ❏ Question and answer
- ❏ Brainstorming
- ❏ Case study
- ❏ Written tests
- ❏ Worksheets and study guides
- ❏ Notebook
- ❏ Open-ended sentences
- ❏ Paraphrase of Scripture
- ❏ Headlines
- ❏ News story
- ❏ Creative writing
- ❏ Outline
- ❏ Word study
- ❏ Diary or journal
- ❏ Quotations

- ❏ Cassette, recordings, CDs
- ❏ Resource persons
- ❏ Listening guides
- ❏ Listening teams
- ❏ Personal sharing or testimony
- ❏ Oral reading such as reading a Scripture passage, a choral reading, responsive reading, dramatic reading
- ❏ Storytelling
- ❏ Circular response
- ❏ Debate
- ❏ Interview
- ❏ Panel
- ❏ Graffiti
- ❏ Singing
- ❏ Writing words for songs
- ❏ Biblical simulation
- ❏ Monologue
- ❏ Dialog
- ❏ Skit
- ❏ Writing drama
- ❏ Games

Reflective

- ❏ Lecture
- ❏ Case study
- ❏ Question and answer
- ❏ Discussion
- ❏ Written tests
- ❏ Worksheets and study guides
- ❏ Open-ended sentences
- ❏ Opinionnaire
- ❏ Attitude scale
- ❏ Creative writing
- ❏ Diary or journal
- ❏ Listening to music
- ❏ Listening guides

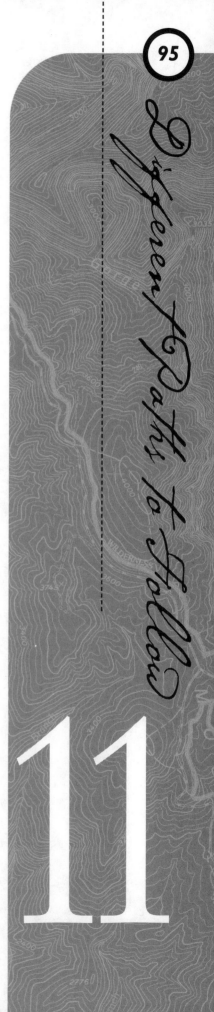

Different Paths to Follow

11

12

by Joe
Sherrer

Over the years my family has taken numerous family vacations. Some of these trips have involved travel through desert regions of the country while others have been where the landscape was lush, green, and dense. In both of these environments—as well as in others—I have found an abundance of plants and animals.

These plants and animals generally have thrived well in the particular environment where we found them. How foolish it would have been to have stated that the ideal environment for a Saguaro cactus was the wet marshes of southern Florida. The more arid Arizona desert is home to this plant, so the marshes of Florida would not have been the appropriate place for this particular cactus.

Providing a good environment for Adult Bible study groups is vital as well. Churches need to provide many necessities for adults—certainly for all age groups—such as good space, resources, appropriate heating, air conditioning, and light. Certainly, adult classes have thrived for decades in less-than-ideal facilities and with minimal resources. At the same time, church leaders need to recognize that people with little or no commitment to Christ and His church seek

places that provide at least a minimum of creature comforts. If our facilities are inadequate, many people will not return after their first visit.

The relationships we establish in the class are important, too. Personal relationships with other followers of Christ help move adults along in their journey of transformational discipleship. Someone has said that just as much is caught as is taught in growing Christian relationships, that we discover how to live the Christian life as we see and hear others living out their walks with Christ.

Each element—let's call them trees—is important in providing the right environment for a transformational Bible teaching ministry. Adult leaders must work toward providing the important and necessary elements that assist teaching and learning.

In our desire to provide the "ideal" environment for Bible study, we sometimes are guilty of not seeing the forest for the trees. The overall spiritual growth process—the forest—is more important than any single element—the trees.

Just as different parts

See The World Around The Path

12

See the World Around the Path

of the country provide different types of environment for a variety of species of plants and animals, different types of Bible study groups and churches may flourish with different elements provided or highlighted. No one approach to Bible study will be adequate for every person.

This chapter attempts to identify the "trees"—the necessary elements of the Bible study process that contribute to the spiritual transformation of learners in Bible study groups. Specific helps for starting and maintaining a Bible study class are provided. However, remember this: The emphasis must be on the overall impact—the successful journey toward transformation within individual adults.

Walking Through the Forest: The Classroom

Perhaps the easiest way to look at the environment in an Adult Sunday School class is to walk along this path looking for two different features: The physical environment of the classroom; and the emotional, relational environment of the class itself. First, let's look at the physical environment of the classroom.

When we're on a family vacation, we can use one of several different ways to get to our destination. We can travel by air; use the old, well-used family car, or rent a van. Each will get us to our destination . . . well, most of them will; the family car was questionable at times. Some ways of traveling are more comfortable; some are more suitable for certain destinations than others; some are more spacious depending on the number of family members traveling together.

SSFNC

Ideas and suggestions for use in weekly leadership team meetings as well as for personal spiritual growth and lesson preparation are included in leader guides.

Bible study group classrooms are something like that. While most any rooms will "work" for Adult groups, some classrooms are more appropriate for certain groups of adults. Some are more comfortable, others are more spacious.

Certainly the principle that people are more important than rooms is true. However, do not minimize the importance of providing a good physical learning environment for adult Bible study groups. The physical room communicates messages about the priorities the church places on ministering to adults. Adults usually have more options than other age groups about whether they attend and where. Today's adults are quite willing to exercise their options—attend, not attend, or go elsewhere—based on whether they are satisfied with the facilities they are given. The image and comfort they perceive from the physical environment contributes to their satisfaction and desire to attend and participate.

The physical room communicates messages about the type of learning activities provided for learners. Participation and involvement are critical aspects of adult education. Participation and involvement also require space. Classrooms should enable teachers and learners to work together toward spiritual growth—toward spiritual transformation. The physical arrangements and facilities may offer a nonverbal message of what leaders expect to happen in a particular place. Chairs in rigid rows neatly arranged in front of a lectern may communicate that learners are to listen but not respond. Chairs in a circle or semicircle may suggest a more open, discussion-oriented style of teaching and learning.

Providing an appropriate physical learning environment is one important step. But a classroom is not defined by material items alone. The learners' perceptions are equally important. To say that the ideal adult classroom should provide so many square feet per adult—a concept of density—is one thing. It is another for people to feel they don't have enough room—a feeling of being crowded. To say the proper temperature should be 65-70 degrees is one thing. It is quite another for people to think the room is too warm—a feeling of being hot. Perceptions are important.

> ## SSFNC
>
> **In selected learner guides, interactive questions and activities are provided that can engage learners in Bible study following the lesson, or can be used during the session.**

Many adults are sensitive to the special needs of adults with disabilities, too. As much as possible, adult classrooms should be barrier free. The ministries and teaching experiences we offer should be available to anyone who wants to attend.

Consider these guidelines for providing space and equipment for Adult Sunday School classrooms:

- Provide 10 to 12 square feet per person in adult classrooms and 8 to 10 square feet per person in department rooms.
- Provide flexibility within the room to vary arrangements of the room from week to week. Room arrangement should be determined by the methods the leader plans to use that specific week rather than methods being dictated by the facilities or room arrangement.
- Whether to use tables or a podium should be influenced by appropriate teaching approaches rather than by tradition or leader comfort.
- When building new classrooms space, consider room shape, lighting and glare, windows, color of the paint for walls, heating and air conditioning as well as ventilation issues, noise and acoustics, placement of electrical outlets, adaptability for technology, wall adornments, style of carpeting, proximity to other age groups of the church and to restrooms, worship center, and fellowship areas. New classrooms should be constructed to comply with the Americans with Disabilities Act, too.
- Equip classrooms with marker boards and tack boards. Provide moveable chairs and tables. If possible, chairs should be padded and should provide good back support.
- In addition to extra Bibles and learner guides, equip adult classrooms with Bible maps, Bible dictionaries, commentaries, and pictures.
- Provide an adequate supply of pencils, markers, paper, poster board, tape, and scissors for classroom use.

Few of us have been fortunate enough to have ideal classroom facilities. No adult leader should feel inadequate or distressed because of the failure to have the "perfect" classroom. Other aspects of the Bible teaching process are far more important. However, remember that the opportunities for good teaching and

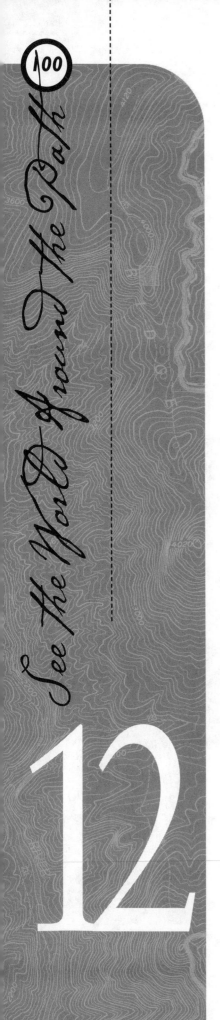

learning in an Adult Sunday School class are enhanced by providing a good physical environment.

The Feel of the Forest:
Emotional and Relational Factors

The environment of an adult Bible study group is made up of far more than physical space and equipment. Ask a group of leaders what contributes to a good environment and you will get a variety of answers. One will say that hospitality is essential for creating a good environment. Another will say that relationships are essential, still others will opt for a positive and encouraging emotional climate.

This emotional climate is impacted by many influences and conditions. Sometimes the emotional climate is influenced strongly by—maybe even controlled by—the teacher or another key leader of the group. Sometimes certain learners control the class by the way they respond to others in the class, to the leader's teaching style, or even to whether emotions are allowed in class. Still other factors that influence the class are cultural in nature.

Guides in the Forest:
Leaders and Their Classes

The phrase "the leader is the lesson" has been established to emphasize the importance of teachers embodying the biblical message. In a similar way, while the teacher of a Bible study group cannot control all relational aspects within the class, the leader does set the tone regarding relationships. Good teaching connects with the needs and interests of learners. But, the relational aspect is just as important. Adult Sunday School teachers must connect with learners in ways that convey friendship, genuine concern, and heartfelt love for each person. Transformational teaching is fostered when teachers establish true personal relationships with learners. These relationships allow for a type of transparency that enables learners to see authenticity and commitment in the teacher's life.

Teachers must realize that these types of relationships do not come easily or quickly. It is not a matter of making a certain number of contacts by telephone each week—although making such contacts may contribute greatly to the process of developing these relationships.

Arriving early each week to talk with members and newcomers is important too, but arriving early to talk does not build the true trust relationship that teachers need to establish. Granted, some vital ministry information can be obtained during this pre-session time. But most people will not express deep personal concerns in the classroom with other people around.

Simply organizing the class with ministry teams—although this should be a basic action—is not enough to build relationships either. To create the type of emotional climate that is crucial to the transformational journey of individual learners requires plugging into the learners' lives. Building relationships becomes a seven-day-a-week learning experience—in fact, a relationship of love.

Leaders also set the tone for the climate in another way: Within the actual teaching-learning process. Within this educational environment, teachers must create a climate of love, trust, and respect not only between teacher and learners, but also among learners themselves. Teachers can help learners grapple with biblical truth and move toward spiritual transformation and changes in all parts of life by respecting their personalities and personal involvement in the teaching experience. No one wants to feel demeaned by sharing a personal struggle or attempt to respond to God's leadership in life. Everyone should affirm and respect the experiences and feelings of others in the class.

Leaders can facilitate this environment in part by showing enthusiasm. The word "enthusiasm" comes from the Greek "to be inspired or possessed by God." Enthusiasm has been defined as having "strong excitement" or having a "feeling in behalf of a cause or subject." Certainly the idea of an enthusiastic teacher as being inspired and possessed by God is vital to transformational teaching.

In general, enthusiastic teachers are those who care about and value their subject matter as well as their learners. Bible study leaders have the most important subject matter—biblical truth—to convey in a life-changing way. The subject matter is more than mere Bible information; it's teaching the Word of God in such a way that lives are changed both eternally and daily. Because of this, teachers should teach in a manner that expresses those feelings with an intent to encourage similar feelings in the learners. Emotion, energy, and expressiveness are vital components in communicating this enthusiasm. Most people respond positively to teachers who teach with a passion for their learners and a passion for the important biblical message.

Bible study leaders also can help create a positive educative environment by teaching with clarity. Although countless volumes of doctrine, history, theology, and philosophy have been written about the Bible, the Word of God is not some ethereal volume given by an eternal Being only to mystify and confuse. God's Word teaches us to love, praise, pray, communicate, respect, reflect, minister . . . I think you see the point.

The Forest and the Trees: Adults in Class

One of the worst words in the English language related to vacations is this: Baggage. On every vacation my family has had we have struggled with what and how much to take. Sometimes we can cram everyone's "I just have to take it" item in the trunk or the car. At other times we have been limited by airline regulations of two pieces of luggage per person plus that which you can "safely stow under the seat of the person in front of you." Regardless of the mode of transportation, baggage also made the trip.

Learners in Bible study groups have to struggle with baggage as well. Whether a later adult group or a young adult class, regardless of whether they are mature Christians who have been growing in Christ for a long time or are people who just recently made a profession of faith, every adult will bring some baggage to the class each week. This baggage will impact the emotional and relational environment of the class.

Some of the baggage participants bring can be characterized as external. For example, adults have family relationships and responsibilities. An ill child can require Mom or Dad to stay home to attend to the child's needs. Virtually everyone understands how this impacts class participation.

Some baggage grows out of relationships among people in the class. Remember that Christians still are human beings, and people simply don't always see things the same way. Conflict and the exchange of harsh words before leaving home to attend Bible study may have a great deal of impact on the emotional climate of the class. The usually compassionate woman who has spent most of the trip to church repairing makeup from an emotional exchange with another family member may not be immediately receptive to the needs and prayer requests of other learners. In a similar manner, secular job responsibilities and changes in employment of learners are very likely to have a direct impact on the emotional health of the entire class. Other community, social, or church relationships and church responsibilities can influence relationships in the class or Bible study group. What appears to be a learner who does not care and fails to invest significant emotional energy in the class may be something else entirely. The person simply may be emotionally tired from compassionate acts of caring at work or in the community. Some adults may be overextended with church responsibilities and other worthwhile groups. They may struggle just to keep their emotional heads above water sometimes. The fact is, external baggage is real and often impacts participation in the class—both during the session and throughout the week.

Participants also are impacted by internal baggage. What appears to be an unwillingness by one person to build close relationships within the class may be the reliving of past friendship failures and an unwillingness to risk again. A sharp comment in the midst of a learning session about a seemingly straightforward issue may be the result of conviction by the Holy Spirit regarding a totally unrelated area of life. This internal baggage may be an unwillingness to deal with a problem or not recognizing a need within one's own life.

Sometimes this baggage comes from a desire for privacy to protect oneself. At other times it comes from an inner commitment to self and family—simply not wanting to overextend to others. Once again, the issue is not primarily whether this baggage is right or wrong. Every learner has these types of internal baggage. The issue is to recognize and manage this baggage because it impacts the emotional and relational environment of the class.

Although usually unpleasant, conflict occurs in a Bible study group from time to time. This conflict may occur during a session because of the learning activities used by the teacher. At other times the conflict grows out of problems that developed between learners during the week. Regardless of the source, this conflict can impact the health of the class.

Within the session, this conflict may be exhibited by a comment expressing a difference in opinion or a wrong answer about one part of the lesson. In such cases the teacher must demonstrate respect for each individual and ensure that all participants are clear about the biblical truth. Inquiring for further information may allow participants to clarify or modify their answers, thus "saving face" and reducing or eliminating further conflict.

At other times teachers may need to study an issue in greater depth and promise to explore the issue later. Sometimes conflict grows out of a negative response to a particular teaching method. Once again, respect individual differences in personality and learning styles. Simply affirm each individual and each learning style, and work with each person to assure a positive learning environment. Choose methods that are acceptable, and make an effort to balance teaching methods so that everyone feels a part of the learning experience. Do not exaggerate a situation by dwelling on a problem during the session. If necessary, deal afterwards with individuals. Do your best to help all learners understand the value of using different methods to teach to different learning approaches.

At other times conflict may arise between learners during the week. In these situations teachers need real spiritual wisdom and discernment. At times ignoring the conflict removes the fuel and the conflict quickly dissipates. At other times swift intervention is the best way to resolve a situation that could spill over into the class. Each situation is different and requires careful attention. Use the following principles as you prayerfully seek wisdom to resolve conflicts in relationships:

- Seek to understand fully the dynamics involved and personal opinions and interests of each person involved in the conflict. Never take sides.
- Realize leadership responsibilities. Sometimes you simply must "step up to the plate" and lead.
- Follow biblical guidelines for resolving conflict. Recall such admonitions as: When your brother has something against you, first go alone to resolve the situation, then if necessary take someone with you. Apply biblical instruction.
- Avoid inappropriate expressions of anger.
- Maintain confidences.
- Keep focused on the overall mission of the class and church. Seek to maintain a spirit of Christian fellowship.

The Forest and the Environment: Cultural Influences and the Class

Today's Bible study groups increasingly reflect our multi-cultural society. Because of the emotional nature of most religious experiences, the cultural dimension may impact the way some adults interact with one another and with the leader. Certainly, economic and educational factors are important when considering the cultural background of learners of the class; but racial and ethnic backgrounds often strongly influence relationships within the class. Various cultures see family structures in different ways. This connects directly with modeling of relationships, too. At issue in different cultures also is communication. This may impact on what can be said and in what way in a Bible study class in different ways. The roles that men and women play in the life of the class may be impacted by cultural background in addition to theological perspective.

Non-verbal communication varies greatly among cultures, especially regarding time and space. Some cultures view time as a commodity that can be wasted, spent, managed, or used. The concept of starting on time is valued and practiced. In other cultures, time is not a concept of concern. In some cultures time moves to the rhythm of nature: the day, the season, and the year. For them, structural inventions such as seconds, minutes, and hours have little or no meaning. With regard to space, people from one culture may be comfortable moving close to one another or touching one another. Some people are huggers, and never hesitate to walk up to another person to give that person a hug.

People in other cultures may be very uncomfortable with someone who constantly hugs them. Hugging is done only within one's biological family, so such hugs represent having their personal space violated. Contact cultures tend to smile, touch, make eye contact, be comfortable with being at closer distances, and be more verbally animated. In short, to be expressive. On the other hand, low-contact cultures tend to stand apart and touch less.

In a similar way, the context of communication varies among cultures. In high-context cultures, communication is laden with numerous contextual clues such as facial expressions, the way something is said, the order people are spoken to, or even what is not said. In contrast, within low-context cultures communication is highly verbal—everything is explained. The verbal message is the message in and of itself.

Two other cultural factors easily may influence the life and ministry of a Bible study group. The people within the class may come from a cultural background where emphasis was placed on being a part of a group. In these "collectivistic" cultures, relating socially and upholding the value of the group are important concepts. One's cultural heritage is important and should be respected. In contrast, other learners may relate more to an "individualistic" culture in which the priority was placed on the choices and personality of each individual.

Another cultural factor that directly impacts the teaching and learning aspects of Bible study is a culture's ability to tolerate ambiguity. Some cultures place a high level on cut-and-dried answers. Something is either correct or incorrect. Other cultures can live with a higher degree of uncertainty, allowing various opinions and options to be considered before determining a final course of action.

Cultural differences add dynamic and flavor to Bible study that can be both exciting and fruitful. However, adult teachers need to consider these cultural factors and how they impact the relationships within the class and the journey toward transformation in the lives of individual learners.

Can't see the forest for the trees? You really have no option; you must see both the forest and the trees! Each adult leader must pay attention to specific aspects that impact the environment of the class or Bible study group. At the same time, avoid getting "hung up" in a particular tree—this rule, this guideline, or this preferred practice. Under the Spirit's leadership, move forward with the mission of the class—a journey of transformational teaching and learning and touching lives with the grace and good news of Jesus Christ.

Joe Sherrer is Professor of Adult Education at New Orleans Baptist Theological Seminary, moving to New Orleans as this book was being completed. Previously he was minister of education, Southern Hills Baptist Church,

12

Part 2
Teaching All the People

THERE'S A REASON WHY we use the word "special" when we talk about adults with special needs. The word isn't just a label intended to avoid a stereotype. Those involved in the ministry to or with special education learners quickly discover that these adults truly are special in the best sense of the word. The many lives touched by these individuals are richer because of it. The vitality of life and the typically unselfish spirit possessed by these adults sets a high and wonderful standard for all believers.

The next part of this book is dedicated to the teacher of adults with special needs. As you'll see, this does not mean it is only for leaders of special education classes. It's for any adult Bible teacher with a heart and passion for teaching the Bible to *all* adults. It is for the transformational Bible teacher willing to lead his or her group to include *any* adult.

Teaching like Jesus means teaching with an understanding that all people are supremely valuable to God. It means being able to look into the eyes of anyone to see the beauty that God sees. If God blesses your life and ministry with the opportunity to teach one or more of these special individuals, then you are truly fortunate. Our prayer is that these pages will help you teach them as Jesus would teach them.

Special Paths for Special People

13

By Ellen Beene

In Jesus' day, there was little love between Jews and Samaritans. In fact, Jews despised Samaritans so much they wouldn't even travel through Samaria, which lay between Judea and Galilee. If Jews traveled to Galilee, they went extra distances to bypass Samaria, going through the barren land of Perea on the eastern side of the Jordan River.

Jesus was different. Jesus chose to travel through Samaria. Because He did so, many Samaritans became believers—their lives were transformed (John 4).

We may not bear the type of animosity the Jews felt toward Samaritans, but many people go out of their way to avoid people who seem "different" from themselves and the people they associate with regularly. Along with people from different cultural and ethnic backgrounds, many people avoid even those within their own culture groups who have some type of disability or handicapping condition. Fear of "catching it," uncertainty about what to say or do, and discomfort lead many people to avoid such individuals altogether.

Is this what Jesus would have done?

The Gospels are full of accounts of Jesus reaching out to and receiving persons with various types of disabilities. Read some of these accounts:

- Matthew 9:1-7
- Matthew 9:27-34
- Matthew 17:14-22
- Matthew 20:29-34
- Mark 2:1-12
- Mark 7:31-37
- Mark 8:22-26
- Mark 9:14-32
- Mark 10:46-52
- Luke 5:17-26
- Luke 9:37-45
- Luke 13:10-17
- Luke 18:35-43
- John 5:1-15
- John 9:1-34

In each passage, a person's life was transformed because Jesus took time to care, to develop a personal relationship, and to lead the person to faith. Adult Bible study leaders are called to do no less. Teachers are called to blaze a path through the Samarias of our time to teach about the transforming power of God.

This chapter is about opening doors to all people who want to be part of the church. This chapter represents a plea against excluding anyone from Bible study because of any kind of disability. No matter how long you have been teaching adults the Bible, this chapter is for you.

Bible study leaders of adults with special needs hold the potential to impact their learners before, during, and after the session just like any teacher. Consequently, they have the same responsibility to *prepare* the ministry environment, *encounter* God's Word, and *continue* the lesson.

Prepare the Ministry Environment

The ministry environment is especially important when dealing with special needs adults. Remember that the ministry environment involves much more than the immediate learning context. It is everything that relates your learners to the group and to one another.

The ministry environment is the total context of the group's work and mission. It is largely relational and recognizes that transformation always occurs in the context of a caring community of faith. For Bible study groups with special needs adults, the ministry environment includes a number of important elements.

Creating Handicap Accessible Paths

Mainstreaming is placing disabled adults in the same class with age-group peers for instructional and social reasons. Doing so also means a place has been estab-

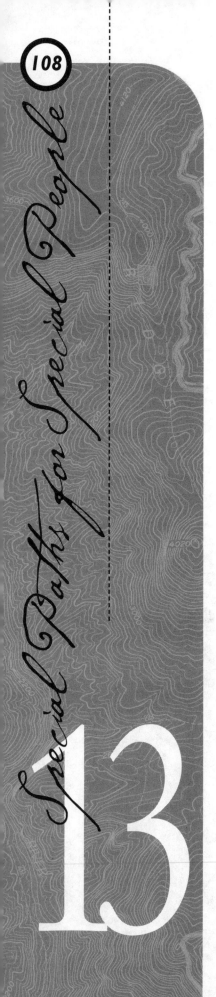

lished for disabled people to benefit from, minister with, and serve beside peers.

Most disabled people can and should be mainstreamed. Most adults who have disabilities can be included in regular Bible study groups. Is mainstreaming important? Think about the difference between welcoming and including someone as opposed to shutting them out. Disabled people fear rejection and the embarrassment of being unwanted and ignored. They want to be welcomed to activities other than just the Sunday morning worship service. Mainstreaming means including people with disabilities in all of our groups and what they do. Looking at our history helps us understand why mainstreaming is important.

Christians intentionally come together for worship and praise. The church should be a collection of people who know the love and forgiveness of God. The church is the only organization whose Founder stressed restoration and complete, unconditional acceptance. Jesus included all people in His earthly ministry. He excluded no one. In fact, He reached out to and accepted people who had been rejected. The church is a partnership of people who trust Jesus as Savior. It is a partnership of people with diverse backgrounds who come together to learn, grow, encourage, and labor together for the sake of the gospel.

No matter where you live or the size of your church family, somewhere in the beginnings of your church was a nucleus of people who came together for worship. That nucleus represents people who worked together, prayed together, and determined to grow bigger. They bonded and developed a common vision. Every addition was welcomed warmly. Then came growth.

Imagine a group of believers who began work less than 60 years ago. In the church's fledgling years, each person was a welcomed contributor. If a person had a disability, so what? The disability was part of that person. In some cases, the disability was a minor drawback that needed to be worked around. The important thing was the person who had joined the ranks.

Church growth and expansion came rapidly; with it came a concern about image. Members wanted star achievers in their ranks, people about whom they could brag. They didn't want people in high, visible positions who were too smart or twisted . . . or impaired. The church wanted to woo and win prospects based on its sharp, average-American image. The focus shifted from inclusion to exclusion, from acceptance to discrimination. Where does your church stand?

Mainstreaming means looking back to where our churches started to see if we strayed off course. Mainstreaming means looking at our purpose and making course changes as necessary. Mainstreaming means seeing people and loving them as Jesus did. He entrusted His followers with the responsibility of reaching all people. Jesus gave those who followed Him the keys to heaven and a charge to invite all who would to come to Him.

When people are asked what the function of a Bible study group is, they often say the group is organized for telling other people about God's love, sharing the good news, leading others to a saving faith in Jesus Christ, or meeting with other believers in a corporate time of worship, praise, and study.

All those answers are true, but not complete.

What if you were asked, Which people? Which believers? Would the answer be the lame, the blind, the deaf, or the intellectually superior? Or do people in

your church modify their responses in subtle, qualitative ways? Does your church really reach out to *all* people?

Mainstreaming means church leaders honestly evaluate how they develop strategies based on what they want to achieve. Mainstreaming means assessing and eliminating restrictions. What limits the outreach plans for your church? What gets in the way of making your Bible study groups accessible to everyone?

Do society's values govern our churches? Is the worth of an individual based on how that person performs? How limited are the perspectives of church members? How do they compare to God's perspective about people? Do members have and admit prejudices? Everyone has some kind of prejudice because people are imperfect human beings. Do adults ask God for the power to overcome prejudices? Do members understand how threatened they feel by things that remind them of their frailties and failures? Do adults know they sometimes are afraid a disability will "rub off on" and contaminate them?

The Americans with Disabilities Act (ADA) became law on July 26, 1990. This legislation provides a national mandate to protect people with disabilities from discrimination and other social injustices. For Christians, the ADA is an example of people getting around to doing what God told them to do long ago!

Bible study groups are in a prime position to model the spirit of the ADA. As organizations, such groups can be social leaders for justice, acceptance, and compassion. Mainstreaming is a tangible way to live what Christians teach. Bible study groups and leaders who openly care about the needs of all people gain the respect of the people around them.

Personal Bible Study

Teachers are the star attractions in Bible study groups. Leaders should point learners' attention to God. Leaders must focus on eternal truths. The fact is, a teacher is a tangible and real presence. Leaders represent all the content they try to teach to learners. In other words, *the leader is the lesson.* Teaching is more effective when teachers:

- mirror God's love and acceptance for each learner.
- show enthusiasm and appreciation for God's Word.
- show the importance of Bible study through well-prepared plans and by being in the room before learners arrive.
- make sure their actions away from church are consistent with what they say at church.
- are open to listening to what each individual is trying to express.
- get involved in learners' lives away from church.
- remember God uses the personalities of all who serve Him.
- acknowledge their teaching weaknesses.

All of these skills, recognitions, and characteristics can be developed as teachers prepare for the session through personal Bible study. This is where teachers are challenged personally by the truth of God's Word. This is where teachers pray for adults they teach as they explore the Bible and prepare for their sessions. This is where teachers' own lives are transformed by personal encounters with the Bible.

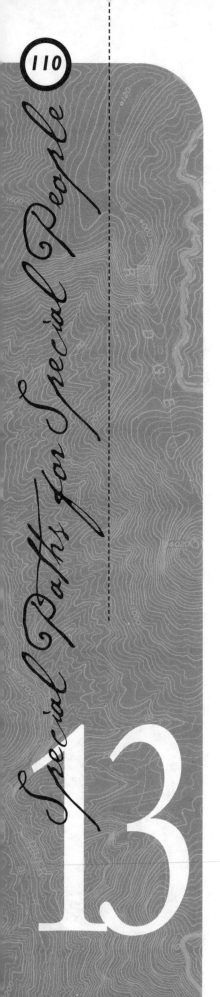

Encounter God's Word

Teaching for transformation with special needs adults is essentially the same as with other adults. Special needs adults need to encounter God's Word just like everyone else. Although their learning paces may vary significantly, disabled people learn in the same ways as other people learn. The seven elements of transformational learning still apply (see pages 72-75 for a detailed explanation of the seven elements).

There are no uniquely successful teaching methods for adults with disabilities. Successful teaching comes from knowing learners individually, learning the strengths and weaknesses of each learner, and knowing how learners prefer to learn. Leaders must know what skills learners have and what activities they find difficult or frustrating. Leaders also must know how to adapt or adjust teaching activities to make the learning environment comfortable and positive.

Adaptation is simply adjusting to a different situation or condition. A wise writer once said, "If you run into a traffic jam on the way to work, you take another route." That's what leaders must do with teaching plans. If a disabled person runs into a road block with one teaching activity, use another. Any challenges in adapting curriculum materials to meet the needs of disabled learners can be minimized as leaders see people with disabilities as people trying to meet the pressures of life and make the most of their abilities despite their disabilities.

Directing Adults with Visual Impairments

Not everyone who has difficulty seeing is blind. Although some adults are born with sight impairment conditions, the major causes of visual impairments among adults usually are linked to aging. With age, the retina degenerates or becomes damaged by glaucoma, cataracts, or diabetes.

A visual impairment is a condition that causes a person's vision to be rated at 20/200 or worse, even with corrective lenses. Having 20/200 eyesight means the person can see at 20 feet what a normally sighted person sees at 200 feet. Vision may be blurred or restricted totally or in part. One person may not be able to distinguish between darkness and light; another cannot differentiate shapes. Central vision (detail and color) may be destroyed or damaged, and peripheral vision may be reduced. Color vision may be defective, especially when differentiating between red and green colors. The ability to adapt from dark to light or light to dark may be slow. Extreme sensitivity to light also may be experienced. *Blind* refers to a person who either has no vision or only the ability to tell darkness from light.

People with visual impairments are not born with more hearing ability than those with normal sight. Any unusual sensory abilities come from early cultivation and practice. Motor development may develop slowly, due in part to the absence of visual cues. People who are blind also may fear falling or getting hurt. Social development may demand more effort because communication often is nonverbal.

To best guide adults who have visual impairments, avoid harsh lighting. Seat them away from the glare of a window. Find out if additional sunlight in the room helps. Find out if you need to shine a desk light on close-up work.

Keep rooms uncluttered and items off the floor. Have a nonskid walking surface. Don't use throw rugs. Help the learner learn the location of items in the room, then keep the room consistent. If you need to move things, inform the learner. Cover sharp corners of furniture. Place bright strips on stair edges.

Provide large-print reading materials, including Bibles and hymnals, Braille materials (when appropriate), audiocassettes, and recorders. You also may need to provide magnifying devices or electronic communication devices such as a Brailled computer, Opticon™, or Tellatouch™.

Do You Know Willie John?

In Vacation Bible School Willie John was the constant energy dynamo. Workers didn't know about learning disabilities back then. They knew little boys his age could be active and fidgety. His speech was not as mature as that of most children, but then, he *was* only five. Teachers would give in, cajole, then get harsh with him, all within three hours. Sunday School, extended teaching care, and elsewhere were the same. His parents brought him to everything.

By the time he reached the Children's Division, he looked for ways to disrupt the boys' class. He didn't like to read aloud. It was too difficult for him, and the other boys laughed when he made mistakes.

As a teenager, Willie John balked at going to church. When he did come, he slouched in his chair at the back of the large-group area, with arms folded and head down. He listened to discussions and occasionally said something, but church was not pleasant for him.

Willie John stopped attending when he got married. He never did overcome the reading difficulty. He feared someone would ask him to read or, worse yet, to teach. But after his children were born, he went occasionally with his wife to worship services. Soon he noticed the church could use his knowledge in sound systems and electronics, and Willie John has served his church in that capacity for many years. No one but his wife knows why he hesitates to be in Sunday School and other small-group classes.

What must we do to help people like Willie John feel that there is a place for them in Sunday School?

Use each of the senses, especially touching and hearing.

Use a combination of activities that require large and small amounts of eye work. Use brightly colored pictures and visuals with simple patterns. Avoid clutter and stripes. Encourage learners to sit as close as possible to visuals. When using visuals, verbalize what learners are to see. Give directions and procedures in simple, clear steps. Make certain learners know the class schedule and inform them in advance about changes.

Use more audio aids than visual aids when teaching a class of adults who have severe visual impairments or who are totally blind. Use discussion and question/answer teaching methods.

Offer assistance for finding a chair, giving written responses, and learning the layout of a room or building. Let totally blind people hold a person's arm at

the bended elbow when being guided around or into a room.

Teachers should look directly at learners and speak in normal tones. Smile and use the same facial expressions used with normally sighted people. Don't avoid words that refer to sight, such as *look* and *see*.

Can You Spot Them?

Learning disabilities are not always easy to identify. Develop an awareness of the potential for learning disabilities by asking some questions that could suggest a learning problem. But remember also that affirmative answers to these questions do not necessarily mean the person does have a learning problem.

1. Is the learner shy?
2. Is the learner disinterested or unaware of what is taking place?
3. Does the learner ask irrelevant questions or give irrelevant answers?
4. Is the learner easily distracted by other activities in the room?
5. Does the learner fail to interact appropriately with peers?
6. Does the learner exhibit disruptive behavior or overreact to what is happening nearby?
7. Does the learner appear frustrated or confused?
8. Does the learner read and understand at a lower level than peers?
9. Does the learner have trouble with oral and written instructions?

Guiding Adults with Learning Disabilities

As much as 10 percent of the population has some type of learning disability. Learning disabilities are caused by a dysfunction in how a person's brain processes visual and auditory information. When teaching a regular adult Bible study group, teachers probably have at least one person who has a learning disability.

Professionals do not agree on one precise definition of learning disabilities. There are as many specific characteristics as there are people who have learning disabilities. Although it is difficult to simplify these characteristics into one typical profile, professionals do agree that people with learning disabilities have normal or higher intelligence; do not achieve academically at the same level as their peers; exhibit low levels of achievement in one or all basic skills of listening, thinking, and memory; have difficulties with one or all basic academic areas of reading, writing, and math; do not have the disability due to emotional problems, visual or hearing disabilities, or mental handicaps.

Professionals also agree that people with learning disabilities exhibit common characteristics of low self-esteem, low motivation, poor concentration, and difficulty in making appropriate social adjustments.

Learning disabilities often are described as hidden handicaps. Adults may not be aware they have specific learning disabilities. They only know the feelings of failure encountered many times in school and other learning arenas. They often feel dumb, are sensitive to criticism (real or imagined), are self-critical, and feel they have nothing to contribute to the group or society. That is where a Bible study group becomes so important in the person's life.

Leaders may not know whether learners have learning disabilities. Even if an adult is aware of a personal disability, that person may hesitate telling their teacher for fear of being labeled as dumb.

To lead adults with learning disabilities, provide a structured, well-organized learning environment. Make certain learners know the schedules and time limits. Be consistent. Limit activity choices and keep time limits short but flexible.

Keep directions simple and clear. Try to use one-step directions when possible. Ask learners to repeat directions to you in their own words to check for understanding. Print multistep directions on a marker board or chalkboard.

Tell learners what to listen for before telling a Bible story or giving a lecture.

Provide an area free of distractions for people who have problems with concentration.

Keep lectures short. Review using an activity that allows learners to move. Keep verbal instructions and commands short, no longer than 10 seconds.

Allow fidgety learners to change seats, take short breaks, or sit closer to friends. This can help learners keep focused.

Develop creative ways to repeat and drill information. Relate all new information to prior knowledge.

Know learners' learning strengths and make certain they have opportunities to use strengths in class. Be generous with praise and positive feedback. Help learners feel safe and not threatened in the learning environment.

Use as many of the senses as possible. Use drama, music, art, and videos in place of pencil/paper tasks. Use visuals and cues to aid attention and memory. Adapt activities that require writing to one-word answers.

Encourage learners to sit close to learning buddies or near leaders and at the front of the room. Provide opportunities for them to work on small-group projects where they can contribute to the team effort.

Start with concrete concepts and move to abstract ideas. Break assignments into small steps. Shorten long activities by asking learners to do only the ones circled or every other one.

Adapt reading activities by rewriting them using words learners know. Be careful not to make this too simple since that can be discouraging. Assign reading buddies to read material orally. Allow learners with learning disabilities to read softly aloud instead of silently. Allow time for learners to highlight words they don't know and to learn them before reading or saying the verse aloud. Restate ideas in simpler terms before learners start to read. Encourage them to use bookmarks as line markers or to help them track as they read.

Leading Adults with Attention Deficit Hyperactive Disorder

Attention deficit hyperactive disorder (ADHD) is not a new problem. People with this disorder have been labeled many ways: disobedient, hyper, and brain

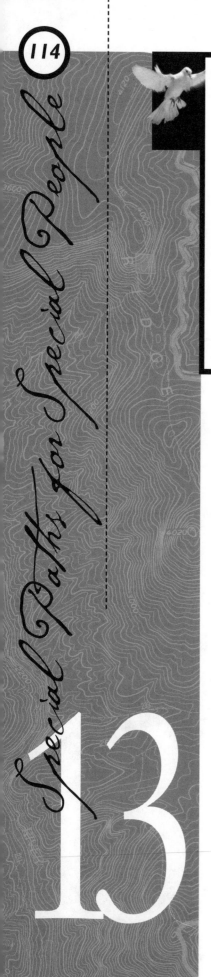

Do You Know Jamie?

Jamie is a young adult with ADHD characteristics. His behavior problems were evident when he was 18 months old. At home and church, he aggressively hurt other children and destroyed property. His parents tried many ways to manage his behavior. They used rewards, talking with him, even spankings. Nothing worked to reduce the problems. Even his siblings did not want to be around Jamie.

By the time Jamie was in high school, he had a history of problems with teachers, academic failures, and rejections. Although gifted and creative, Jamie was able to finish high school only in an alternative school setting. He does not attend church at all. Members of his youth group made Jamie the brunt of too many jokes and comments.

Jamie does not believe Christians can show love and understanding since he seldom received that from Christians. How can we help Jamie?

damaged, for example. When leading adults who show ADHD traits, help them find their strengths and encourage them to use them. Maintain good communication with them. Listen when they talk. Provide a structured learning environment, but allow them to have some ownership in decisions that affect them. Provide positive feedback, meaningful rewards and consequences. Create a learning environment with short breaks and opportunities for active responses. If you need to talk with learners about inappropriate behavior, do so privately.

ADHD is a pattern of hyperactive-impulsive behavior and/or severe and persistent inattention behavior that is evident early in life, and often continues into adulthood. Some of the observable behaviors include:

- Lacks sustained attention.
- Makes careless mistakes.
- Does not listen when spoken to directly.
- Cannot follow instructions.
- Does not organize tasks.
- Dislikes and avoids tasks requiring sustained mental attention.
- Loses work materials.
- Is easily distracted.
- Forgets daily activities.
- Fidgets or squirms in seat.
- Displays restless, excessive, or inappropriate movement.
- Cannot remain seated.
- Cannot wait for others to complete their turns.
- Does not take part in leisure activities quietly.
- Acts as if "driven by a motor."
- Talks excessively.
- Blurts out answers before questions have been completed.
- Interrupts or intrudes on others.

Adults Who Are Gifted

A gifted adult has significantly above-average intelligence or talents that require special attention to nurture and develop. Not all gifted adults are successful. Some fail because they are not interested in what is happening in a classroom experience and have a disdain for routine, ordinary tasks. Some gifted adults who are not challenged and who already are familiar with lesson content may cause problems. Other gifted people quietly resign themselves to the boredom, but do not stay long with the situation.

People who truly are gifted display rapid learning in early childhood. They can give long spans of attention to topics that interest them. They are quick to see how that topic relates to their lives or another topic, which is part of their ability to quickly grasp cause-effect relationships. Gifted people display a high degree of curiosity. They frequently are involved in a variety of projects at one time. Gifted people are more likely to be well-informed on a variety of topics. Their problem-solving abilities enable them to take facts (the general) and apply those concepts (the specific). Because gifted people expect much from themselves and others, they often are most interested in social topics such as social reform, politics, and religion.

In Bible study, realize that gifted adults do not readily accept what they consider "pat" answers. They see outside the lines of tradition, ask challenging questions, need to be encouraged to develop spiritually inquiring minds, and need to hear the spiritual inadequacy of all persons is met in the person of Jesus Christ.

People who are intellectually bright have the potential to think deeply. They

---

Do You Know Sarah and Kyle?

Gifted adults may have faced problems with teachers and others in Bible study. Do you know someone like Sarah and Kyle?

"I hated having teachers who got offended at my questions. They acted mad at me for being smart. I guess it made them feel uncomfortable."—Sarah

"I didn't like class at first because all the guys wanted to spend their time talking about this one girl. I happened to know her at school, and I knew her reputation wasn't the best. But there was one other guy in the class who wanted to know more about the Bible too. Our teacher worked so hard to make the class interesting for me and the other guy that I kept coming back."—Kyle

How can we make Bible study groups more responsive to people like Sarah and Kyle?

---

also have the potential to influence, encourage, and lead others. Because some gifted adults are not encouraged to develop their gifts at church or because they do not get the answers they seek, some may give up on Christianity for meeting their spiritual quests and leave the church.

Gifted adults experience frustration because they live in a world in which others may not understand the way they think or the motivation and drive

13

behind the things they do. Gifted people have trouble developing close friendships. They are not readily accepted because their thoughts run ahead of their peers. At times, expectations put on gifted adults are too simple and therefore discouraging. Other times expectations can be too much, bringing overwhelming demands. Often gifted people feel distanced from the average world.

Teaching adaptations need to be made for gifted adults. Welcome their questions without feeling threatened. If you don't have an answer, say so. Encourage learners to design a Bible-learning project related to their questions. Provide books and resources for use outside of class that speak to the biblical or historical content of the question. Appoint study teams to investigate a topic. Use learners' abilities to articulate through writing, music, or other creative forms. Encourage them to express the whys and hows of an issue or topic. Offer choices. Plan a learning environment that allows freedom to study. Ask thought-provoking questions that address concepts and real-life applications. Encourage problem solving by using analogies, comparisons, brainstorming, and creative thinking. Use creative teaching techniques such as drama, creative writing, puzzles, or game show formats that keep the learner interested and involved.

Encourage talented learners to share their talents, but don't pressure. While thinking about the talents and gifts or bright minds, remember the gifts and talents of all learners. Encourage each learner to develop his or her talents and gifts. Look for ways to affirm each learner and plan for each to have time in the spotlight to shares thoughts and abilities.

Help people with leadership potential know how to serve. Use case studies of biblical characters, great names in church history, and profiles of people in your community to show that good leaders first know how to serve others.

Avoid giving gifted learners preferential treatment. This can cause resentment in other learners. Provide opportunities for positive social interaction between gifted learners and peers.

As with all learners, help gifted learners focus on knowing and pleasing God, learning to evaluate their strengths and improving their weaknesses, and learning that even when we cannot control or answer all of life's mysteries, we can control our own responses to circumstances and to God.

Clear the Path for Adults Who Have Physical Disabilities

Nothing says welcome more than visible evidence. If guests can find a place to park and an easy-to-enter entrance, they feel less hesitant to enter. Nothing says welcome more than a building that is accessible to physically disabled people.

Many churches and public buildings now are aware of the architectural barriers that keep people with physical disabilities from coming into that building. Most new building codes require accommodations for wheelchairs and other orthopedic aids. Churches with older buildings can survey their facilities to determine how accessible their buildings are. That may include basics such as reserved parking, wider halls and doors, accessible rest rooms, curb cuts, ramps, and elevators. (A sample survey is included on the CD-ROM in the Leader Training Pack.)

Physically disabled adults should have access to all parts of the church. Ask a

"Where's the elevator, please?"

Vacation Bible School is a popular summer event in most Southern Baptist churches. A mother came to one Southern Baptist church for the Family Night activity during VBS.

"Where's the elevator?" the mother asked one worker after getting out of her van. She was near the entrance to the two-story building in which VBS was conducted. The woman was in a wheelchair.

The worker directed mother and family to the door into the building and helped them find the elevator, easily visible in a main corridor. The mother seemed impressed with the accessibility of the facilities for people with disabilities, both inside and outside the building.

How well can people with physical disabilities navigate your facilities?

---

person in a wheelchair to assist in evaluating the accessibility of all church buildings. After completing the survey, share and evaluate results with church members, set goals to remove barriers, publicize and celebrate achieving each goal, and publicize your church's accessibility with the International Wheelchair logo in newspaper and phone book ads, church brochures, and on your church sign.

Bible study rooms should be located and arranged for easy access and maneuverability. Make certain people have enough room to maneuver around furniture with a wheelchair or other mobility aid. Rest rooms should be located as closely to the room as possible.

Wheelchairs need to fit beneath table edges, or lap boards need to be provided. Shelves, drawers, sinks, hangers, or hooks should be within easy reach. Floors should be made of slip-resistant materials that wheelchairs, scooters, and walkers can maneuver on easily and that provide shock absorbency.

Unless learners have additional disabilities, they do not require different teaching procedures from peers. Adapt for needs.

Know about disabilities. Read. Ask professionals. Ask the person. Don't be afraid to ask questions. Learn about assistive equipment they may use.

Make certain people are positioned comfortably and properly. Positioning refers to assistance learners may need to lie down, sit, or stand comfortably and still best use their abilities. Each disability has its own positioning requirements. Positioning may be as simple as providing a different type of chair or a pillow, or as complex as knowing how to arrange learners at body-support tables.

Know that learners may need more time to complete an activity.

Never do for physically disabled people what they can do for themselves.

Accept disabilities while focusing on individuals and their strengths.

Encourage them to use talents and gifts.

Don't equate physical disabilities with mental disabilities. Talk directly to people. Respect their levels of understanding. *Do not* talk down to them.

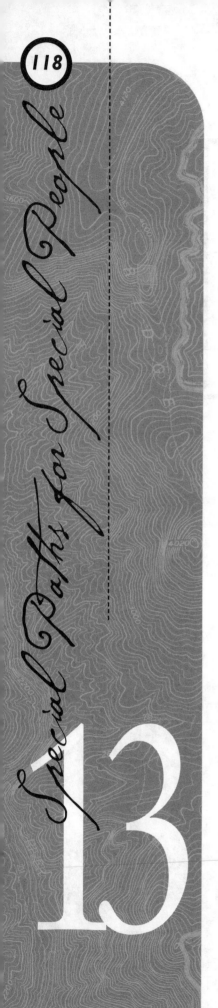

Know that people who have become physically disabled as a result of an injury or illness deal with stress and grief. Provide ministry appropriate to each person's need and ability.

Taking a Separate Path

By the time learners with mental disabilities reach adulthood, the gap between their intellectual development and those of age-group peers may have become so great they may not learn as much in a regular class. Creating specific classes for some older youth and adults may work best. Some adults with mental disabilities are married. Those couples may want to attend their regular age-group classes, and every effort should be made to help them do so successfully.

Some young adults whose handicaps are less complicated or extensive may want to attend classes attended by peers and other adults of their age group. This will work if other learners are sensitive and supportive. All attempts should be made to include higher functioning young adults and older youth in the social and recreational activities of their age groups.

Each person is unique and should be given the opportunity to choose what class to attend whenever possible. If some adults are unable to blend in well with adults who do not have mental limitations, be sensitive and caring. Provide distinctive classes for people as appropriate. Encourage without being abrasive or condescending to adults who may not fit in with other adults.

Be as familiar with individuals with mental retardation as you are with others in the class. Generally, there is a qualitative difference in the way people with mental disabilities see the relationship between concepts and the degree to which they can handle abstract concepts. Adults need concepts expressed in simple or concrete terms. People with mild mental retardation may have no distinctive physical appearance that would suggest a difference from other adults. Most are marginally independent, and often are described only as "slow." They may have difficulty paying attention, communicating verbally, demonstrating memory skills, being self-motivated, or demonstrating social skills.

Adults with moderate mental retardation often have difficulty with abstract ideas, transferring what they have learned to a new situation, and communicating. They may be emotionally immature and have underdeveloped self-concepts. They may achieve success in self-help and social skills, but require supervision. They may have physical traits that cause them to appear "different."

People with severe or profound mental retardation are likely to have additional handicapping conditions. They may be unable to communicate with intelligible speech, to walk, or to care for their personal needs. They may fail to respond to physical or visual prompting, but tend to respond more rapidly when taught one-on-one. They develop quite slowly, and are dependent and require constant supervision.

Mapping a Positive Learning Environment

People with mental handicaps respond best to a structured—but not rigid—learning environment. Part of that structure not only follows a consistent teaching schedule that provides a secure routine but also allows for flexibility.

Maintaining a good leader-learner ratio is part of developing a positive learning environment. Whenever possible, try to follow these ideal ratios of workers to participants:

- 1:1 for severely disabled learners, with no more than 6 per group
- 1:4 for higher ability learners, with a limit of 15 learners per group
- 1:2 or 1:3 for persons with skills in between, with up to 12 per group

At least two leaders always are needed in every class for people with mental disabilities, preferably one male and one female. All leaders should know what to do in case of medical emergencies. Get first-aid training through the American Red Cross or talk with workers in area group homes about where their house managers get training. Before you begin such a class, check with your church staff about limitations on church insurance issues. Be certain you know the medical alerts and concerns of all learners. If learners come from an intermediate care for mentally retarded adults facility (ICFMR) or if a medically fragile learner lives at home, plan to have a nonteaching assistant, familiar with specific medical needs, to be in the room at all times.

Navigating the Encounter

A typical Bible study session should last about 60 minutes. One schedule suggestion that works well includes:

Capturing learners' interest (10 minutes) involves activities that help learners prepare to learn. These activities often are highly creative and fun and can be conducted in large groups. In many instances this is where learners will be guided to acknowledge authority and deal with *control*.

Searching the Scriptures and understanding their truths (25 minutes) represents the core of the session. Remember: The Bible is the textbook for the study. Use the Bible in teaching experiences. For this time, learners most likely will meet in small groups based on skill and understanding levels. Guide learners to explore biblical *content* as well as understand its *concepts*.

Personalizing, struggling with, and believing Bible truths (20 minutes) is the session segment during which leaders help learners realize how the Bible relates to their lives. Activities can be very personal and are best done in small groups or individually. Here learners will address *context*, *conflict*, and *conviction*.

Closing the session (5 minutes) brings the session to a gradual halt. It provides time for a reverent finish and transition to worship or extended teaching care. This segment also provides an opportunity for leaders to challenge learners to allow the Bible truth for the day to become a matter of personal *conviction* and transform their lives.

Scouting Out Learning Activities

The old saying, "Involve me, and I will understand," is especially true for adults with mental disabilities. Like most of us, they will remember more if they learn by discovery. Learning activities are those direct, purposeful experiences that allow opportunities to retain what they see and hear.

The key to using teaching activities rests on what teachers know about the unique mix of learners' skills and abilities. Not all learners can do the same

activity the same way. Consider each learner's skill level; then group learners according to skills and plan activities for each group.

Do You Know Susan and Ernie?

Susan is a young woman who grew up in the church where I was a member. She attended regular Sunday School classes until we formed one for adults with mental handicaps. Because she had mild mental retardation, Susan joined the new class. Susan drove her own car, held good community-based jobs, and handled her own money. I asked her if she was comfortable in our class and reminded her that she had the choice of attending a class with other young adults. I knew the department would welcome her. She declined, saying she knew she was different from those adults. She learned more in our class for adults with mental handicaps.

Ernie, on the other hand, did not grow up in that church. He also had mild mental retardation and visual disabilities. He tried to attend the regular class for young adults but did not have the social skills that helped him be accepted into that group. Some of his behaviors were disruptive and inappropriate for his age. The same department that would accept Susan was not sensitive to Ernie and did not want him there.

Activities should meet these criteria:

- *Be age-appropriate.* Is an activity one that all adults would do? Adults with mental disabilities do not want to be treated as children. Wilda and her husband came to Vacation Bible School for adults. They knew their limitations, but were proud of their jobs and marriage. The VBS teacher asked each person in the group to make handprints on white paper. Wilda started to cry. She was frustrated. "I'm 35 years old. I don't want to do baby work."

- *Relate activities to content.* Do teaching methods relate to the emphasis and biblical truth for that session? Every song, picture, and game must be a tool that helps learners focus on content. Adam's teacher wanted him to know that God gives us good food to eat. Because Adam is nonverbal, his teacher asked Adam to point to simple pictures of fruits and vegetables, and she planned a game about making good food choices. When they had a healthy snack, the teacher thanked God for good food to eat and led Adam to nod for his amen.

3. *Be relevant.* Biblical truths must be relevant to what is going on in learners' lives today. If lives are changed and transformed and if teachers help learners apply Bible truth to everyday living, then content must have meaning for the things that are happening now. Jenny wanted her class to remember that God is with us when we are afraid. Jenny asked a learner to name a time when he is afraid. She then led that learner to thank God for being with him at that time.

When planning activities, consider:

- the purpose of the activity and how it relates to the purpose of the session.
- space and resources.
- time requirements (Do you need to enrich, shorten, or do preliminary

steps? Will the activity frustrate or bore learners?)

• variety of activities planned for each session

Some activities will need to be adapted for learners to grasp some concepts. Keep these ideas in mind when adapting activities.

1. Know learners well. Know how each learns and the skills each can use successfully without frustration.

2. Think of adaptation as an adjustment to fit learners' needs, not as a complete overhaul.

3. Use common sense.

4. Allow learners to do everything they can for themselves.

5. Slow the pace.

6. Express concepts in simple terms. Provide real-life examples and concrete experiences. Give only one concept at a time.

7. Plan for extra individual attention.

When introducing new activities or concepts, be brief. Present each step in sequence. Be aware that you may need to back up and present a step again. Make success possible in each step. A good rule of thumb is: Repeat. Repeat. Repeat. Repeat. Repeat . . .

Present a concept in a variety of ways. Make applications to situations learners will know. Reduce sight and sound distractions. Introduce new vocabulary words before telling new stories. Provide an outline of important points. Use pictures and other visuals with all activities. Use materials that are of high interest and low difficulty level.

Many adults with mental handicaps read on a low level or not at all. Adapt for them by using pictures; recording instructions on an audiocassette; using diagrams and line drawings; using color coding, shape coding, number coding, or texture coding; placing a pattern over important words to help with word search and crossword puzzles; using role play, music, and movement activities.

Some learners are not able to communicate verbally. Work with learners who have difficulty communicating by using a system that works for each learner. Use gestures, sign language, a picture board or book, even an electronic communication device. Ask questions that can be answered by nodding or shaking the head. Use signs mounted on dowel rods—green circle for yes, red circle for no. Provide nonverbal ways learners can participate in singing (play a rhythm instrument) and drama (pantomime parts). Use visual activities and pictures that require learners to point, follow broken lines, or match symbols. Did you know that 70 percent of all communication is nonverbal? Use skills you already have to understand nonverbal learners and talk to them as though they can respond verbally.

What is the key word for guiding adults with mental disabilities along spiritual paths? Abilities. Emphasize what each learner is able to do, what you are able to do to help that person learn better, and what God is able to do in that person's life because of your willingness to know and teach that person.

Special Paths for Special People

13

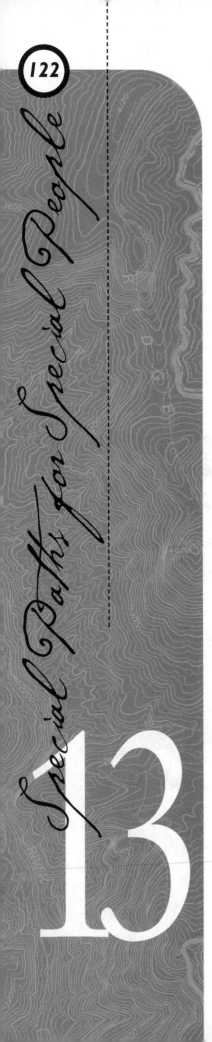

Lead with Storytelling

Because telling the Bible story is the major activity in Bible study groups, leaders should prepare for teaching all week long. Many people think telling the Bible story is merely that—telling the story by lecturing. Granted, the lecture is the foundation for telling a story, but lectures can be varied and adapted in ways that will keep learners attentive and interested. Make lectures more productive first by breaking lectures into several minilectures, and then by using varied voice inflection, understandable vocabulary, visual aids, familiar instructions, good eye contact with listeners, good time limits, well-developed questions, and appropriate activities. Use all of these each time a Bible story is told to people with mental disabilities. Even people with profound mental disabilities, who may not seem to comprehend what you're saying, can benefit.

Involve learners in a variety of ways when telling a Bible story. Make the story the most enjoyable learning activity of the session.

Use open Bibles. Provide an easy-to-read Bible (3rd- to 6th-grade reading level) for each learner. Direct learners to open their Bibles to the Scripture passage each session. Mark their Bibles before the session begins.

Present the basic facts. Show a large biblical picture. Tell the story briefly the first time. Consider this example for 1 Samuel 3:1-10: Today we will hear about Samuel. He lived with Eli the priest. One night Samuel heard someone call his name. Samuel thought it was Eli, but Samuel learned that God was calling him.

Go into greater detail. Let learners choose to tell the story themselves, ask someone to portray the key character (Samuel tells the story in first person), or involve learners in a drama (provide biblical costumes or hand puppets and a script). This tells the story a second time.

Keep the content short. Do not tell everything you know. The Bible story should not last more than three to five minutes. Before the session begins, leaders should know what they are going to say and stay with their selected points. Even learners with higher abilities cannot handle great theological discussions.

Review the facts. Adapt at least one activity to review the highlights of the story. Ask: Did Samuel live with Eli the priest? Was Samuel alone in his room that night? Did Samuel hear someone call his name? Did Samuel say, "Speak, Lord, for Your servant is listening"? Write questions that learners can ask the man who portrays Samuel; ask volunteers to tell the story using the biblical picture. This tells the story a third time. Even with this much repetition, learners may not have short-term recall about the story.

Make a transition statement. Refer to the Bible story during the application activities. Say: God had a message for Samuel. Samuel listened to what God said. God has a message for us today. We can listen to God's Word.

Evaluate how Bible stories most often are told. Is the vocabulary appropriate? How are learners involved? Do activities match each learner's skill level? Are activities age-appropriate? Are stories presented in more than one way? Are they interesting? Are illustrations relevant to learners' lives?

Guide Through Sign Language

Moving day had arrived. We were heading for our new home! We were busy

unloading boxes. We already knew the son of one of our new neighbor's was completely deaf. My husband looked across the lawn. Before I knew why, he was at the neighbor's front door.

"How do you sign 'watch for cars'?" he asked the mother.

She started signing, "Watch for . . . " and abruptly stopped. "Where is he?" she shouted. My husband pointed to the street in front of the house. Scottie was racing his big-wheeled bike as fast as he could go, oblivious to anything around him. He wasn't watching for cars or his mother. She ran to the street and pulled Scottie and the bike into the driveway. As fast as her fingers could fly, she said, "Young man, I've told you. Stay out of the street. Cars can kill you."

That was the beginning of our intrigue with sign language. By the way, Scottie's mother showed us other "applied hand communication skills" that day.

Our country has a fascination with sign language. American Sign Language (ASL), or Ameslan, is reported to be the third-most-used language in the United States. Sign language is a visual gesture language developed by deaf people to communicate with one another.

But sign language is not just for deaf people. In the expressive hand pictures of sign language, people learn to hear with their eyes and speak with their hands. This communication language is logical and concrete, using more than one learning modality. Many people with mental disabilities, who cannot speak otherwise, are able to communicate with simple signs. Other people with mental disabilities, who otherwise are verbal, love to sign because it is a most complete and expressive way to communicate.

Becoming proficient as a signer takes time, but people with even a casual interest in signing can learn basic concepts and signs in a short time. A large number of well-illustrated learning guides show how to make signs and explain the concept or memory aid associated with each sign. Sign language is a versatile teaching tool, and creative leaders can find many ways to use it.

Introduce vocabulary. Work one-on-one with severely disabled learners. Point to people and objects either in the room or in a picture. Demonstrate the sign slowly. Help learners practice signing by pointing to an object and saying the word. Create interest in the session. Practice the sign for an important word that learners will hear throughout the session, or learn signs for new words that learners will hear in the Bible story.

Sign the Bible verse. Print a short Bible verse on a sheet of poster board. Put an enlarged sign language illustration under each word. Lead the nonreading learner to "read" the verse with sign language. Teach learners the signs to a Bible verse as a tool to help them memorize the verse.

Use signs on a rebus. Substitute the pictures in a simple rebus with the illustrations of familiar signs. Note that most songs and choruses repeat words and phrases to help emphasize the main concept in the song. Use illustrations of signs in place of the repeated words and phrases when making a song chart.

Sign songs. Learners enjoy signing favorite songs. Help people learn the signs to favorite hymns. Learn new signs weekly. Look for repetition of many signs throughout the hymns. This activity builds sign vocabulary quickly.

Lead learners to write a praise to God using signs they know. Use a familiar tune.

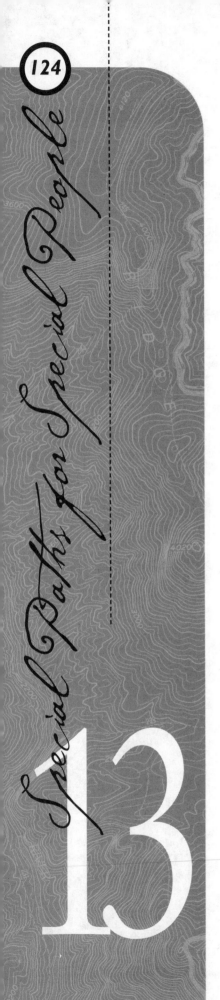

Direct them as they sign and sing their praises. If learners are part of a special education choir, make certain they sign one of their songs each time they perform. At least once each year, arrange for learners to sign while the worship choir sings a special song. Invite other members of the congregation, including any who are deaf, to practice and perform with learners.

Prepare a long-playing videotape. Feature an interpreter signing as a soloist sings familiar hymns. Use these videos to plan an individual activity.

Sign prayers. Encourage nonverbal learners to pray in sign language as someone prays aloud. If someone needs help praying, show how to sign each word as the speaker voices a simple prayer.

Lead learners to write a group prayer on a large sheet of paper. Direct as the group reads and signs the prayer together.

Ask volunteers in the large group to say: I praise God because He is (fill in here). Ask learners to complete the thought in sign language.

Sign a Bible story. Ask volunteers to summarize, using sign language, the Bible story. Use simple vocabulary words to write a drama about the Bible story. Direct as volunteers speak their parts with sign language. Ask a learner to read the verbal interpretation. Arrange for an interpreter to sign the Bible story each session to learners who are deaf.

Direct Through Music

"I can't sing."

"We don't have a piano in the room."

"None of us knows how to lead songs."

Excuses . . . that's all these are! Many more can be added to this brief list. Unfortunately, too many leaders don't feel comfortable using music in class. Are they self-conscious? Do leaders imagine they have to be highly talented musicians? They don't, really. People with mental handicaps are among the most accepting of people. They don't mock or tease or even notice if you sing off key. But they do enjoy singing and participating in musical activities.

Music has been described as the language of the soul. Music stirs emotions and causes a response from each of us. People with disabilities respond to music the same ways as people without disabilities. And why not? People cannot respond incorrectly to music. There are no wrong answers or hard questions. Music is positive. Whether you like one type of music or another is a matter of personal taste. But music itself offers a chance to grow and expand. Music offers adults with mental disabilities opportunities for self-expression and positive attitudes. Music is a tool that can help us remember and communicate.

As you think about the ways you use music with learners, remember some basic principles.

Many nonmusical activities can involve music. Music can accompany the class on a walk around the room or provide a background as learners plan a party. Leaders often sing instructions or praise learners for appropriate behavior with simple tunes.

Music provides a way for learners to feel part of the group. Even nonverbal or multidisabled learners can move with the music, play a rhythm instrument, or take part in a game.

Music is an avenue for creative expression. Leaders use music to help nonverbal persons express moods. (Show me how you move when you are sad, happy, tired, hungry.) Learners who are frustrated or noncompliant can express their feelings by playing a musical instrument.

Music can be used to reinforce a learning activity and stimulate imagination. Learners can sing Bible verses, role-play songs, and answer questions with musical sounds. They even can learn to listen for the music in nature, such as singing birds, gentle breezes, falling rain.

Music is a gift from God to help us express praise, know about the world and people around us, and be aware of the bodies God created for us to use. Again, leaders do not need to sing well or know fundamentals of music. The key is that leaders use music in each session; indeed, leaders can use music more than one way in any one session.

Musical experiences can be rhythm, singing, using instruments, or body movement. The potential for using these in the teaching session is unlimited. Consider these examples.

As you *capture learners' interest,* lead them to clap a steady 1-2-3 rhythm. Play a recording relating to the Bible story. For example: modes of travel (the people of Israel travel to a new land) or sounds of nature (God made the world).

Teachers can sing a welcome with a simple tune as learners arrive, then use the same tune to sing an introduction to the Bible story. Learners can sing with leaders each time. Learners can play cymbals or tambourines as they prepare to learn about Bible-time worship. Learners also can listen to a recording of African rhythm music as learners take a nature walk.

As you guide learners to *acknowledge authority, search the truth* and *discover the truth,* ask learners to hum to the rhythm of the Bible verse. Call on volunteers to make up songs as they retell the Bible story. Direct nonverbal learners to play shakers or small bells as others sing. Direct learners to sway to the music as they sing a song related to the Bible story.

When guiding learners to *personalize the truth, struggle with the truth, and believe the truth,* guide them to speak in rhythm: Thank You, God. Thank You, God, for our homes and our jobs. Thank You, God. Ask volunteers to locate a song from a hymnal that relates to the session truth. Lead learners in a "wave" to express their willingness to obey God this week. Help learners play a tune on an autoharp to express their responses to God's call on their lives this week.

As you close the session, guide them to *obey the truth.* Help learners gain self-control with an ageless rhythm and hand movement: Roll them, roll them, roll them, roll them. Give a little clap. Roll them, roll them, roll them, roll them. Lay them in your lap.

Use familiar tunes as learners sing and shake hands with one another: Shake a hand, shake a hand of a friend. Shake a hand. Please, don't be shy. Shake a hand, shake a hand next to you. Now it's time to say good-bye.

Who leads the singing in your class? What do you use for instrumental accompaniment? Play a recording of quiet music. Say, This music reminds us to be quiet and respectful of others in the worship center.

Ask other church members to help with music. This small responsibility does

not require the same preparation as teaching, yet allows others opportunity to work in your class and still have time to be in their own classes. Having other church members accepting small class assignments unearths hidden talent and encourages people who never dreamed they could minister in Bible study groups. It frees your time for other responsibilities in the class, too. If you are uncomfortable singing in front of groups, enlisting other adults solves your dilemma.

Ask learners or other people in your church or community to help occasionally or for special projects. You may be surprised at the number of people who are willing to help during one session each month or for an entire month. Youth have great musical and other skills, too. Remember to ask them occasionally.

Consider using different types of instrumental accompaniment. Learners often enjoy a variety of instruments to accompany songs. Use recordings, a guitar or other stringed instrument, keyboard, drums, handbell, cymbal, tambourine, wind instrument, shaker, hand chimes, or soprano xylophone.

Learners may have such serious disabilities that they do not tolerate loud and unusual noises. Use soft sounds on the keyboard; sew small bells on the corners of washcloths; fill cylinder-shaped containers with fine sand; play soft recordings; add other gentle-toned instruments. Be certain you introduce each instrument one at a time so learners can adjust to them.

Blaze a Prayer Trail
As a teaching tool, prayer helps us realize God is a person who loves us and is interested in our daily concerns. He helps us learn to express our thoughts and

Do You Know Steve?
Steve is paranoid and anxious much of the time, even when he's taking his medication. The anxiety and paranoia are part of his mental illness. He enjoys Bible study because he feels secure and loved there. One day Steve agreed to pray aloud, and the tenderness in his voice amazed everyone. Steve didn't ask for anything; he just praised God: "Jesus, You are so sweet. God, You are kind. God never hurts me or makes fun of me. I love Him. Amen."
Who was the teacher in that moment?

feelings, and causes us to realize true strength and power exist outside ourselves.

Leaders of people with mental disabilities can use prayer in one-on-one teaching experiences to help individuals regain control and prepare to hear a Bible story. Leaders can pray with learners who use a communication board as a way to respond to biblical truths. Prayers help learners feel they are part of the group and teach them about worship, praise, and thanksgiving.

Leaders can use prayer in ways other than listing prayer requests. Reinforce a Bible truth or Bible verses through prayer. Ask learners to thank God for their Bibles. Learners also can share about the fun and exciting things that happened in the previous week through prayer. Stop to give learners a chance to thank God for special experiences and teach them to praise God.

Point to Bible Verses

Teachers often display Bible verses for learners to read and "learn" each week. They do an activity and then go on to something else. Learners may be able to say the verse at the end of the session, but have they really learned something?

Remember to guide a discussion about the content of verses when they are presented. Ask questions about the verse. Explain what the verse means and ask learners to repeat what you said. Call on learners to tell what they think or feel as a result of hearing the verse. Refer to the verse during the application time. Help learners transfer truths from the verse to what they are being taught.

Whether teachers have a different verse each session or one for an entire month, learners need to memorize Scripture. Creative assistance from teachers can make the challenge easy and even fun. In addition to sign language and music, illustrate each word with a symbol, shape, or picture. Use an easy-to-read Bible translation for easier words. Draw or cut pictures and symbols from outdated Bible study materials. Print the Bible verse on a card strip. Lead learners to place the words in sequence. Illustrated verses benefit learners who are visually impaired, especially if the illustrations include texture with the shape that they will touch. Blind individuals learn to identify words with shapes. Guide them to put the shapes in sequence as they say the words.

Guide learners to write poems with the verses. Create or adapt a game to play with each verse. Print each word on matching color cards and play a game such as Concentration. Print the verse on a large poster and cover a different word each time you lead learners to say the verse aloud.

Record each learner on an audiocasette or video tape as each person says the verse alone. Lead learners to say the verse as they hear their voices played back to them when the recordings are played for the group.

Search for Puzzles

Puzzles are fun and are popular learning activities that are appropriate for people of all ages and skill levels. Puzzles involve multisensory stimuli, so they help us learn and retain what we have learned.

Adults with mental handicaps often like the challenges of puzzles, especially ones with built-in success. Most puzzles can be adapted to a learner's level of functioning without embarrassment to the learner. Puzzles can be used to teach a Bible verse, review a Bible story, or as an application activity.

Make a cut-apart puzzle for the low-skilled nonverbal learner. Print a Bible verse or yes-type question with the answer on, or glue a picture to, heavy paper or poster board. Cut the item into three large jigsaw shapes. If learners need a guide, position the puzzle on a large sheet of poster board and draw an outline of each piece. Use this as a one-on-one activity. Puzzles can be cut with diagonal, straight, or angled lines as well as in jigsaw shapes.

Make a texture-coded puzzle for visually impaired learners. Print review statements on separate card strips, then cut each into two pieces. Glue matching textures (fabric or sandpaper, for example) to the back of each pair. As learners match the pairs, read each part of the statement to them. Puzzles also can be coded by number, sound, shape, or color.

Modify a word search puzzle for nonreaders. Highlight the words in yellow and read each word as a learner underlines it with another color. An alternative is to cover the puzzle with a pattern that shows the hidden words. Written puzzles can be coded puzzles, acrostics, crosswords, or fill-in-the-blanks.

Never wonder whether puzzles are used too often. Many learners want to work some type each week. Well-adapted puzzles are a secure and comfortable activity for easily frustrated learners.

Watch for Pictures

A pictures always has been a universal way to communicate. We learn to identify pictures in books before we read and understand words. In special education classes, use three basic types of pictures:
- Biblical teaching pictures relating to the content of the Bible stories
- Real-life teaching pictures relating to true stories or situations
- Activity pictures that help learners review Bible facts, learn a Bible verse, or apply a biblical truth

Leaders and learners alike can have fun using pictures in unlimited, creative ways. Consider several ways to use pictures in class:
- Feature pictures in a unit display.
- Direct learners to imagine they are people in the picture. Ask what they would feel or think in that situation. Lead learners to pose like the picture.
- Make a chronology of a Bible hero's life.
- Build a creative writing assignment around a picture.
- Illustrate the meaning of a Bible verse.
- Create a gallery or unit wall of pictures to tie several sessions together.
- Make a pictorial song chart for the nonreader or a puzzle so learners can "read" parts of the story.
- Use simple pictures to introduce and build vocabulary or word recognition.
- Feature a "learner of the month" and display pictures about that person's life. Keep a class album of interesting projects, fellowships, parties, and trips.
- Make games by using sequenced pictures, matching activities, or puzzles.
- Ask learners to express what they feel or know by drawing pictures.

Curriculum resources most likely will provide all three basic types of pictures each session, both in learner guides and on colorful posters. Look for supplemental activity pictures in previously published materials, especially adult Bible study materials. Use large biblical teaching pictures from outdated leader packs and ask children's workers for permission to use pictures from their files. Often they will allow other teachers to use or duplicate them. Consider purchasing a set of children's Bible study teaching pictures for use with adults with special needs, too.

Remember to select pictures that contain age-appropriate content for adults. Be careful that real-life pictures do not show adults making poor or compromising choices. Choose pictures that are uncluttered and not visually "busy" so learners can tell easily what is happening in the pictures.

Discover Arts and Crafts

Arts and crafts are big items in many special education Bible study groups. The value and appropriateness for using them often is debated.

Who is right? What do you think?

Bible study groups are organized to teach the Bible and lead lost people to Jesus. All curriculum materials should aid leaders in achieving these goals. Materials chosen for Bible study groups also should respect the age and abilities of learners; materials never should place learners in a position to be ridiculed. Help learners learn in ways acceptable to adults.

Help adults with mental handicaps realize biblical truths are for their everyday lives. Do arts and crafts keep learners from achieving those goals? Merely for the sake of doing arts and crafts, they are not valuable choices. As teaching tools or relevant projects, arts and crafts can be well-developed instructional choices.

Many experienced teachers say their learners, representing a wide range of skills and abilities, do not want to do craft projects in Bible study groups. These adults attend work activity centers and community-based jobs and are accustomed to doing what other adults do. They seem to be selective, agreeing to some art activities but balking at others.

How successful teachers guide their classes varies. Corella, for example, has taught a special education Bible study group for 30 years. She is a loving and compassionate teacher who knows her learners and spends time with them away from church. Many members have been in the class from its beginning, starting when they were children. Most of them are nonreaders and nonverbal. Some still live at home with older parents and do not attend a work program of any kind. Corella says her learners expect a coloring activity when they arrive for Bible study. In fact, the schedule has not changed much over the years. Learners sing the same songs and tell the Bible story in much the same way. Corella finds this is less disturbing to learners and helps them feel secure.

Jim doesn't do crafts in Bible study. He thinks crafts will make adults with mental handicaps look childish and open them to ridicule. But Jim likes to do the craft projects at special education retreats. Jim is exceptionally good at woodworking and enjoys the challenge of modifying wood projects the participants can use at home. He says that while learners work with him, he can catch many teachable moments to relate biblical truths to their lives.

The preferences of other teachers fall somewhere between that of Corella and Jim, using arts and crafts on a once-in-a-while basis. At times, teaching plans suggest a craft or art activity or leaders know activities that will help learners understand truth. But crafts are not used every week. Instead, special education leaders choose to use arts and crafts in Vacation Bible School, for missions projects, for Christmas parties, for activities to illustrate biblical truths or relevant applications in extended teaching care, during scheduled arts/crafts/game nights, or in displays and bulletin boards.

If you do use art and craft activities, keep several tips in mind.

• Use felt-tip markers or colored pencils rather than crayons.
• Use glue sticks instead of glue.

Special Paths for Special People

13

- Use modeling clay rather than play dough.
- Use colored chalk, water-color pencils, and other supplies you might find in an art store.
- Plan projects that can be completed in one session.
- Complete preparations that require power tools before the session begins.

Do You Know Jack?

Jack is a 43-year-old man with mental disabilities who attended a retreat. He could not read many words, and this embarrassed him. The first time he was asked to take part in a drama activity he was hesitant. Finally he whispered his fear: "They'll find out I can't read."

He did not need to know how to read. In fact, most of "them" could not read either. We practiced a choral reading. Jack had one short line to memorize, which he said perfectly. He held his paper as if reading the line. Jack did a great job and his face glowed with pride. His leaders said Jack talked about that skit for 12 months. The next year at our retreat, Jack was the first to ask whether we were going to do another skit.

- Always allow learners to choose activities and don't expect every learner to want to participate in every project.
- Provide puff paints, fabric paints, glitter, and other textured mediums for three-dimensional projects.

Clear a Path with Drama

Drama can be used every session. If you doubt there is a bit of a "ham" in each of us, attend one of our special education retreats. Some people who have never spoken and who exhibit all types of delayed social responses take small roles and put their hearts and souls into their parts. It's wonderful.

Drama helps people identify with other people and their feelings. Drama helps adults put on the mask of another personality and exhibit a boldness we can't display at other times. Drama is a multisensory activity and can help people learn more quickly and retain information longer.

Drama is a team effort, too. It helps us learn to work in a group and to appreciate each member's contribution. Drama can be used in each part of a teaching session and can be combined with other teaching methods such as art, music, sign language, or creative writing. Drama preparation can require time to write a script or can be impromptu. Drama can be a narrative, a group reading, spoken parts, or a pantomime. Learners enjoy them all. You can use drama as a role play to create interest, when a guest tells the Bible story from a first-person perspective, to review the Bible story through a picture pose or acting out the Bible story, as learners apply Bible truths by acting out real-life situations they have written.

When using drama, follow these general guidelines:
- Assign roles based on learners' skills and abilities.
- Plan for readers, nonreaders, and nonverbal learners to be involved in some way.

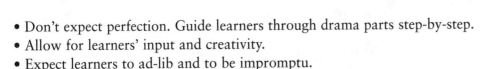

- Don't expect perfection. Guide learners through drama parts step-by-step.
- Allow for learners' input and creativity.
- Expect learners to ad-lib and to be impromptu.
- Practice, even if the "performance" is brief and that same day.
- Don't limit the size of the cast. You can have one actor if you have a class of one, or you can have two or three groups presenting the small skit if you have a large class. If your class is large, vary the activities used in the skit. For instance, one group can pantomime Samuel hearing God's call; the next group can do a choral reading; another can interview Samuel and Eli about the call. Include leaders in the drama when possible.

Continue the Lesson

Spiritual transformation likely will not occur during a one-hour Bible study session. Real transformation may require years for the seeds leaders plant in a given Bible study session to nurture, grow, and transform a learner's life. A learner may struggle for years with the idea of forgiving others before truly experiencing the freedom and peace forgiveness brings. The Bible truth learners repeat at the close of a session may be completely forgotten by the next day.

SSFNC

A complete list of special education resources is included in the Appendix of this book.

So, as a Bible study leader, your job does not end at the close of the Bible study session. In truth, the close of the session marks the beginning of a continuing process of teaching adults what the Bible says and leading them toward spiritual transformation. To help learners experience transformation, leaders must be involved in learners' lives beyond the Bible study experience. Leaders must know what is happening on a daily or weekly basis. They must know learners' concerns about home, work, family, relationships, health, and so on.

To continue the lesson outside the Bible study environment, follow up after each Bible study session, talking with learners about how they are incorporating session truths into their daily lives. Mail postcards reminding learners of their weekly Bible verses. Invite learners to a prayer luncheon at their job sites. Involve learners in ministry and mission projects. Do whatever you can to help learners realize living a Christian life is a 24/7 responsibility, not simply how they conduct themselves during the Bible study session.

Ellen Beene is editor, Adult VBS-Ventures Section, Adult Sunday School Ministry Department, LifeWay Church Resources, Nashville, TN, and attends Belle Aire Baptist Church, Murfreesboro, TN. The content of this chapter has been adapted from A Place for Everyone, *by Athalene McNay.*

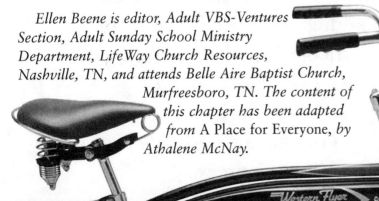

Part 3
Teaching Tools That Transform

THIS BOOK IS ABOUT TEACHING the Bible for transformation in the lives of adults. It is based on the conviction that teaching the Bible should be more than dispensing information about the Bible. It requires a broader context of personal leader preparation, ministry, and prayer as God's Spirit works through the Bible study group to bring about transformation in the lives of both the leader and learners.

The book has been structured to be helpful to any adult Bible teacher who desires to teach for spiritual transformation. For this reason, most of the book is targeted to any Bible teacher and doesn't assume any particular kind of curriculum. It assumes, however, that the majority of readers will be Sunday School teachers or teachers of evangelistic Bible study groups. Therefore, the SSFNC sidebars and certain segments are provided to address the specific needs of adult Sunday School leaders, particularly if they are using Sunday School for a New Century (SSFNC) resources released by LifeWay Christian Resources in the Fall of 2000. The following Appendix has been designed to provide even more specific information about these resources.

NEW CENTURY RESOURCES

Teaching for spiritual transformation is the theme of this book. In that context it deals with a variety of subjects, ranging from the characteristics of a leader to the nature of a Bible study lesson. There is, however, one simple value uniting all of the chapters—the importance of God's Word in transforming lives.

In a sense, chapter 5 is the heart of the book. It is in chapter 5 that we explored the principles of teaching for spiritual transformation. *Use the Bible* is the first of those principles. This principle affirms the value of Bible study materials and supplemental helps in assisting learners and leaders in Bible study. Not meant to replace the Bible, Bible study materials offer users helps for encountering life-transforming Bible truths and for understanding and assimilating those truths into life.

Beginning with the Fall of 2000, LifeWay Christian Resources of the Southern Baptist Convention offers two dated series of resources for adults to utilize in ongoing, open Bible study groups—Explore the Bible and Family Bible Study. The following pages provide descriptive information on these two series and their resources. This information can help you evaluate which series is best for adults in your church. (Note: In the interest of ongoing improvement and refinement, descriptions are subject to change after the Fall of 2000.)

As you consider the benefits of these resources, you need to keep in mind that all of these products have been designed to reflect and support the teaching and ministry philosophy contained in this book. This points to an important principle: **Your church's Bible study ministry and strategy should be defined first and then should determine the nature of your curriculum resources, not vice versa.** Before you select curriculum resources you should determine what it is you want your Bible study strategy to accomplish, then select resources that will help you achieve that goal. For example, if you want your Bible study groups to be open and evangelistic, you should not select resources that assume all participants are believers who will commit to a long term study.

As you study the series characteristics, ask: Would adults in our church benefit more from a study plan that addresses life issues and is organized around biblical worldview questions or from from one that offers a systematic study of all the books of the Bible? Would adults in our church prefer to study a churchwide, common theme or a distinct adult study based on the books of the Bible? Would the adults in our church benefit more from closely-graded groups or non-graded groups?

Materials in the two series fall into these categories—learner guide, leader guide, leader pack, and supplemental helps that vary from audiocassette to commentary to interactive study guide. There also are general adult resources that support both series. As you study these descriptions, ask yourself these questions: Would adults in our church prefer Bible study resources based on the New International Version or the King James Version of the Bible? Would adults in our church prefer lessons they use in preparation for the Bible study session and during the session or lessons they use during the Bible study session and then again in continuing the lesson after the session?

There are two key things you need to know about learner guides and leader guides as you approach the use of Bible study materials from LifeWay Christian Resources, effective with the Fall 2000 quarter.

- Learner and leader guides utilize either a before-during or a during-after approach to the session. The before-during approach assumes learners prepare/study the lesson prior to attending the Bible study session and provides related in-session, interactive elements. The during-after approach assumes the learner makes no preparation of the lesson prior to attending, calls for involvement of the learner during the session, and provides "continue" activities for use beyond the session. Both approaches are interactive in nature, but take a differing approach to learner preparation and study, which then impacts how the leader teaches the lesson.
- Leader guides focus on helping the leader with his/her own spiritual growth and preparation for teaching as well as providing Bible commentary, teaching helps, life application ideas, and ministry ideas. If leaders are to be the lesson, then they must first be transformed themselves by the truth before they can facilitate transformation in the lives of their learners.

EXPLORE THE BIBLE SERIES

BIBLE STUDY PLAN

- A systematic study of all books of the Bible in ways appropriate to the needs of adults
- Bible study plan covers all 66 Bible books and is based on the nature, structure, and content of the Bible as a whole and of Bible books

BIBLE STUDY APPROACH

- Adults study a Bible passage and theme distinctive from other age groups

PUBLISHING CYCLE

- Resources are dated and released quarterly

AGE GROUPING

- Non-graded (all adults)

BIBLE TRANSLATION

- Based on New International Version
- Bible text is printed in both NIV and KJV for easy cross-referencing

LEADER RESOURCES

- One Leader Guide for all adults
- Adult Leader Pack
- Supplemental resources include a separate commentary and *Biblical Illustrator*

LEARNER RESOURCES

- Convenient-sized book with full-color cover and 2-color inside pages
- For preparation **before** the session and group Bible study **during** the session
- Learner Guide also available in large print or on audio tape
- Interactive Study Guide also available

DEVOTIONALS

- Separate quarterly devotional guide: *Open Windows*
- Separate monthly devotional magazines also available for women *(Journey),* men *(Stand Firm),* and new Christians *(Believe)*

USE OF COLOR

- Two-color Learner Guides
- Two-color Leader Guides

In the interest of ongoing improvement and refinement, series descriptions for all Bible study resources are subject to change and/or modification after the Fall 2000 quarter. For the latest information, consult the LifeWay Church Resources Catalog, call 1-800-458-2772, or visit us at http://www.lifewaysundayschool.com.

FAMILY BIBLE STUDY SERIES

BIBLE STUDY PLAN

- Includes a balanced study of Bible books, people, doctrine, history, and classic Bible passages
- Study plan is organized around biblical worldview questions and addresses life issues

BIBLE STUDY APPROACH

- All ages use a common Bible study theme each week with common passages as often as suitable

PUBLISHING CYCLE

- Resources are dated and released quarterly

Closely Graded	AGE GROUPING	Non-Graded
• Closely-graded (ages 18-24; 25-39; 40-59; 60-74; 75 & up; Collegiate Young Adults; Single Adults; Special Education)		• Non-Graded (all adults)

Closely Graded	BIBLE TRANSLATION	Non-Graded
• New International Version		• New International Version • King James Version

Closely Graded	LEADER RESOURCES	Non-Graded
• Separate Leader Guides for each age group 18-24; 25-39; 40-59; 60 & up • Leader Packs for ages 18-24, 25-39, and 40-59 include a CD-ROM with leader helps • Adults ages 60 & up Leader Pack • Supplemental resources include *Biblical Illustrator,* Hobbs and Advanced commentaries, and Bible studies on audio tape		• One KJV Leader Guide for all adults and one NIV Leader Guide for all adults • Adult Leader Pack • Supplemental resources include *Biblical Illustrator,* Hobbs and Advanced commentaries, and Bible studies on audio tape

Closely Graded	LEARNER RESOURCES	Non-Graded
• Convenient-sized books with full-color cover and full-color inside pages • 18-14, 25-39, and 40-59 for use **during** the session and **after** the session to continue the study • 60-74 and 75 & up for preparation **before** the session and group Bible study **during** session		• Convenient-sized books with full-color cover and 2-color inside pages • For preparation **before** the session and group Bible study **during** the session • KJV Learner Guide also available in large print or on audio tape

Closely Graded	DEVOTIONALS	Non-Graded
• Collegiate, Single Adult, 18-24, 25-39, and 40-59 Learner Guides include daily devotional features • Separate quarterly devotional guide: *Open Windows* based on a weekly theme • Separate monthly devotional magazines also available for women *(Journey),* men *(Stand Firm),* and new Christians *(Believe)*		• Separate quarterly devotional guide: *Open Windows* based on a weekly theme • Separate monthly devotional magazines also available for women *(Journey),* men *(Stand Firm),* and new Christians *(Believe)*

Closely Graded	USE OF COLOR	Non-Graded
• Full-color Learner Guides • Two-color Leader Guides		• Two-color Learner Guides • Two-color Leader Guides

Resources	# of Colors Inside	Size of Book	CD-Rom in Pack	Bible Translation Version
Family Bible Study Series				
FBS: Adult Learner Guide NIV	2	5 3/8 x 8 1/8	N/A	NIV
FBS: Adult Leader Guide NIV	2	8 1/8 x 10 7/8	N/A	NIV
FBS: Adult Learner Guide KJV	2	5 3/8 x 8 1/8	N/A	KJV
FBS: Adult Learner Guide KJV, Large Print	2	6 1/4 x 9 1/2	N/A	KJV
FBS: Adult Leader Guide KJV	2	8 1/8 x 10 7/8	N/A	KJV
FBS: Adult Leader Pack	4 & 2	N/A	No	NIV-KJV
FBS: Single Adult Learner Guide	4	7 x 9	N/A	NIV
FBS: Collegiate Learner Guide	4	7 x 9	N/A	NIV
FBS: Young Adult Learner Guide	4	7 x 9	N/A	NIV
FBS: Young Adult and Collegiate Leader Guide	2	8 1/8 x 10 7/8	N/A	NIV
FBS: Young Adult and Collegiate Leader Pack	4 & 2	N/A	Yes	NIV
FBS: Life Answers Learner Guide	4	7 x 9	N/A	NIV
FBS: Life Answers Leader Guide	2	8 1/8 x 10 7/8	N/A	NIV
FBS: Life Answers Leader Pack	4 & 2	N/A	Yes	NIV
FBS: Life Truths Learner Guide	4	7 x 9	N/A	NIV
FBS: Life Truths Leader Guide	2	8 1/8 x 10 7/8	N/A	NIV
FBS: Life Truths Leader Pack	4 & 2	N/A	Yes	NIV
FBS: Ventures Learner Guide	4	6 x 9	N/A	NIV
FBS: Pathways Learner Guide	4	6 x 9	N/A	NIV
FBS: Ventures and Pathways Leader Guide	2	8 1/8 x 10 7/8	N/A	NIV
FBS: Ventures and Pathways Leader Pack	4 & 2	N/A	No	NIV
FBS: Access Learner Guide	4	8 1/8 x 10 7/8	N/A	NIV
FBS: Access Leader Guide	2	8 1/8 x 10 7/8	N/A	NIV
FBS: Access Leader Pack	4	N/A	Yes	NIV
FBS: Advanced Bible Study Commentary	1	6 x 9	N/A	NIV
FBS: The Herschel Hobbs Commentary	1	6 x 9	N/A	KJV
FBS: Sound Truths: Bible Studies on Tape	N/A	N/A	N/A	NIV
FBS: Adult Audiocassette	N/A	N/A	N/A	KJV
Explore the Bible Series				
ETB: Adult Learner Guide	2	6 x 9	N/A	NIV-KJV
ETB: Adult Learner Guide Large Print	2	7 x 10 1/2	N/A	NIV-KJV
ETB: Adult Leader Guide	2	8 1/8 x 10 7/8	N/A	NIV-KJV
ETB: Adult Commentary	1	6 x 9	N/A	NIV
ETB: Adult Study Guide	2	6 x 9	N/A	NIV-KJV
ETB: Adult Cassette Tape	N/A	N/A	N/A	NIV
ETB: Adult Leader Pack	N/A	N/A	No	NIV-KJV
General Adult Resources				
Biblical Illustrator	4	8 1/8 x 10 7/8	N/A	N/A
Special Education Today	2	8 1/8 x 10 7/8	N/A	N/A
Open Windows	1 & 4	4 1/8 x 6 1/4	N/A	KJV
Open Windows, Large Print Edition	1 & 4	5 3/8 x 8 1/8	N/A	KJV
Open Windows, Audiocassette Edition	N/A	N/A	N/A	KJV

Target Audience	Lesson Emphasis Sequence	Devotional Elements in Learner Guide
All Young Adults & Adults	Before-During	No
Leaders of All Young Adults & Adults	Before-During	N/A
All Young Adults & Adults	Before-During	No
All Young Adults & Adults	Before-During	No
Leaders of All Young Adults & Adults	Before-During	N/A
Leaders of All Young Adults & Adults	N/A	N/A
Single Adults	During-After	Yes
College Students	During-After	Yes
18-24 Young Adults	During-After	Yes
Leaders of 18-24 Young Adults	During-After	N/A
Leaders of 18-24 Young Adults	N/A	N/A
25-39 Adults	During-After	Yes
Leaders of 25-39 Adults	During-After	N/A
Leaders of 25-39 Adults	N/A	N/A
40-59 Adults	During-After	Yes
Leaders of 40-59 Adults	During-After	N/A
Leaders of 40-59 Adults	N/A	N/A
60-74 Adults	Before-During	Yes
75-Up Adults	Before-During	Yes
Leaders of 60-Up Adults	Before-During	N/A
Leaders of 60-Up Adults	N/A	N/A
Young Adults & Adults who have mental handicaps	During-After	Yes
Leaders of Young Adults & Adults who have mental handicaps	During-After	N/A
Leaders of Young Adults & Adults who have mental handicaps	N/A	N/A
Young Adult & Adult leaders/learners desiring additional in-depth commentary	N/A	N/A
Young Adult & Adult leaders/learners desiring additional in-depth commentary	N/A	N/A
Young Adult & Adult leaders/learners desiring audio NIV content	N/A	N/A
Young Adult & Adult leaders/learners desiring audio KJV learner guide	N/A	N/A
All Young Adults & Adults	Before-During	No
All Young Adults & Adults desiring large print edition	Before-During	No
Leaders of All Young Adults & Adults	Before-During	N/A
Leaders of All Young Adults & Adults	N/A	N/A
Young Adult & Adult leaders/learners desiring an interactive study guide	N/A	N/A
All Young Adults & Adults desiring audio learner guide	N/A	N/A
Leaders of All Young Adults & Adults	N/A	N/A
All Young Adults & Adults & Leaders of Young Adults & Adults	N/A	N/A
Leaders or families of persons who have mental handicaps	N/A	N/A
All Young Adults & Adults & Leaders of Young Adults & Adults	N/A	N/A
All Young Adults & Adults & Leaders desiring large print edition	N/A	N/A
All Young Adults & Adults & Leaders desiring audio edition	N/A	N/A

Sunday School for a New Century Scope Areas

"Scope" refers to the acceptable limits of study for a curriculum plan. In the truest sense, the "scope" of an adult Bible study group is the Bible itself. This, however, is much too broad to help those who develop the study plan for Bible study curriculum. Consequently, the following five scope areas have been developed to guide those who develop study plans for *Sunday School for a New Century* resources.

- Bible Books. The original, intended message of the Bible book.
- Bible People. Individuals or groups who played a recorded role in the biblical revelation.
- Bible Doctrine. Major themes occurring in the Bible such as salvation, faith, grace, obedience, and so forth.
- Bible History. The plot, eras, and events which frame the historical context for the divine revelation.
- Classic Bible Passages. Passages or books with a fairly specific didactic purpose. Examples could include the Sermon on the Mount, the Ten Commandments, Paul's writings to the churches, prophetic sermons, and so forth.

These scope areas should not be perceived merely as approaches or types of Bible studies, though they may parallel a variety of different kinds of studies. The intent is to reflect the divine pattern of objective, recorded revelation. In order to encompass the full scope of the Bible, we must understand how God has spoken to us through the written Word. In the Bible, God chose to speak through recurring themes (Bible Doctrine). God chose to speak through real events in history (Bible History). God chose to speak through the lives of real people in real life (Bible People). He chose to speak through authors who recorded unique and varied messages from a variety of times and places (Bible Books). God chose to speak through very specific, recorded teachings which are intended to convey timeless principles and absolutes (Classic Bible Passages). The scope categories above reflect this divine pattern of revelation.

These scope areas reflect a structural pattern rather than a theological pattern. That is, they reflect how the Bible is structured rather than a doctrinal paradigm. This is important because the Bible is comprehensive in nature; that is, it touches all aspects of life. Because the Bible is comprehensive, a model that follows a structural pattern will also come closer to being comprehensive.

Family Bible Study

The Family Bible Study series will provide a balanced study of all five scope areas identified above. In addition, the Family Bible Study curriculum plan development process is guided by the goal of helping learners adopt a biblical worldview (see chapter 4). In order to achieve this, all 12 elements of the biblical worldview will be explored and dealt with in some way each year. Some will be addressed more than others in any given year. Nonetheless, churches can be confident that in the course of any given year (September through August), learners will have the opportunity to participate in Bible studies that explore each of the fundamental biblical truths essential to the biblical worldview.

Each lesson will raise and be linked to Relevant Life Questions that in some age-appropriate way arise out of the Fundamental Life Questions and the Universal Life Needs of people. Each lesson, week by week, will seek to help learners grasp in a clearer and stronger way some further aspect or explanation of the Foundational Biblical Truth of one or more of the Biblical Worldview Categories. In this way, each lesson, unit, and study theme will help believers, in a way relevant to their lives, adopt and develop the biblical worldview.

Explore the Bible Series

The Explore the Bible series provides a systematic study of all books of the Bible in ways appropriate to the needs of adults. The study plan will cover all 66 Bible books and is based on the nature, structure, and content of the Bible as a whole and of Bible books. Due to the nature of the series, Explore the Bible series will focus on Bible books in its basic structure. It will, however, in the context of each book, explore Bible people, themes, history, and classic Bible passages.

Teaching Plan for
Teaching Adults: A Guide for Transformational Teaching

General Preparation

Teaching Adults: A Guide for Transformational Teaching has been written to provide you with a navigational aid to take you to a new level of teaching effectiveness as you lead adults toward spiritual transformation. Adults who come to Bible study have spiritual needs that call for the touch of the Master. God has placed in your hands the opportunity to shape and guide adults to become more like Christ. That opportunity comes with great responsibility and accountability. James 3:1 sets out clearly that God expects our best when we teach. Teaching is more than technique, too. Biblical teaching is shaping lives to become more like Christ.

This book can help you lead Bible study teachers to become transformational teachers . . . mentors, guides, and equippers who take adults to places they may never have gone before in Bible study experiences. But you must make a personal commitment to "raising the bar" in your own personal Bible study and your teaching effectiveness. If you are not committed to becoming a better teacher, then teaching this study will lack the enthusiasm and sincerity needed to guide others to a new level of effectiveness.

These suggestions included here are designed for two hours of teaching. They are structured to be used either as 10 minievents of about 10-12 minutes each in regular Sunday School leadership meetings or as a single, 2-hour training plan. Note that the Leader Training Pack includes a videotape. This teaching plan calls for brief segments of the tape. The rest of the videotape segments can be used in additional weekly leadership team meetings to help teachers get a better understanding of learning approaches and the teaching methods that can be used with each learning approach. **This entire tape is not to be used in this two-hour event.** Additional teaching suggestions are included in the Leader Training Pack for more extended teacher training. You will need to identify portions of the videotape to be used in this session.

Create a thematic learning environment for the event. Obtain appropriate items for a hike, trip, or outdoor adventure. Note the theme ideas at the beginning of each chapter for ideas. Items like hiking gear, camping equipment, a globe, life jackets, a compass, and so forth could be used to suggest the direction of the training experience. Local sporting goods stores may have items like topographic maps and other items for effect. Integrate the thematic ideas in each chapter as you develop portions of each teaching step.

Arrange the room so everyone can see a focal wall clearly. Make sure the video equipment is placed in an appropriate location so everyone can see and hear well. Preview the videotape and the CD ROM for material you want to use in the teaching plan. Some of the materials in the Leader Training Pack can be used in subsequent training opportunities during leadership team meetings or in personal work with individual teachers as well as in the extended teaching plan.

If you plan a 2-hour event, get off to a good start. Welcome participants as they arrive. Give each a name tag and call attention to the resource table. Ask them to get a marker and make a name tag. Provide an icebreaker for participants to complete while you continue to greet people as they arrive. Use one that causes participants to move around the room while talking to other participants. Provide a time of debriefing and conversation related to the icebreaker to help participants develop a group atmosphere.

If you are leading the training as 10 separate minievents, explain how the training will occur. Provide a calendar that indicates what dates these segments will be taught. Indicate that each procedure is intended for 12-15 minutes, and that additional time in the leadership team meeting will be devoted to usual portions of the meetings. Close each session with a prayer of commitment, asking God to help workers seek new ways of teaching based on the content of that session.

Preparation for Specific Procedures

Procedure 1—This procedure calls for the video from the Leader Training Pack. Preview the video in advance. Note that the introduction segment is a dramatic monologue of observations the apostle Peter might have made as he watched and listened to Jesus teaching and touching lives. Prepare a marker board or a large sheet of paper for the brainstorming activity. Prepare the poster "Biblical Worldview Model" Chart (Kit Item 10).

Procedure 2—Prepare a poster based on "Five Essential Traits for Effective Teachers." If you have the Leader Training Pack, a PowerPoint presentation of these traits and the elements of the section, "The Price of Leadership." If possible, use this presentation to illustrate content for this procedure.

Procedure 4—This procedure calls for the Kit Item 13, "7 Guiding Principles for Spiritual Transformation." If you do not have the Leader Training Pack, prepare a simple poster on a large sheet of paper of these principles. Also be prepared to distribute plain sheets of paper for the reflection activity.

Procedure 6—Prepare the *Prepare* part of Kit Item 12, "Prepare, Encounter, Continue." This procedure calls for Kit Item 8, "Benefits of Weekly Leadership Team Meetings." If you do not have the Leader Training Pack, make a list of the benefits. An explanation of these benefits can be found in chapter 5 of *Adult Sunday School for a New Century,* by Richard E. Dodge and Rick Edwards. A brief Powerpoint presentation on the primary benefits of a weekly leadership team is included on the CD-ROM.

Also included on the CD-ROM is a Powerpoint presentation entitled, "Developing Listening Skills." Kit Item 7 in the Leader Training Pack can be used as a listening sheet with this presentation.

Procedure 7—Prepare the *Encounter* part of Kit Item 12, "Prepare, Encounter, Continue."

Procedure 8—Prepare the *Continue* part of Kit Item 12, "Prepare, Encounter, Continue."

Procedure 9—Be sure a video player and and monitor are available for this procedure. Before the session, cue up the tape to the segment you want to show to participants.

Procedure 10—An Acrobat document is included on the CD-ROM with the Scripture passages listed at the beginning of chapter 13. If you are not equipped to print the document from the CD, mark each Scripture on a separate 3 x 5 inch card, to be distributed as indicated in the procedure. Prepare copies of "Accessibility Survey" form (Kit Items 5 and 6) for this session.

Procedures

1 Say, Jesus demonstrated that teaching for transformation is more than teaching merely to retain facts. If you have the Leader Training Pack, introduce and use the first segment of the videotape. If you use this segment, reduce slightly the time increments for each action that follows in this step.

Explain "teaching for transformation" based on chapter 1. Then lead a brainstorming activity (3 minutes) to list instances when Jesus taught for transformation. Point out that people need teaching that changes their lives more than teaching that merely informs their minds.

Ask: Did the way people viewed the world change after encountering Jesus? Give a minilecture (3-5 minutes) on how we need to develop a biblical worldview, based on chapter 4. Use Kit Item 10 to help participants understand the elements of a biblical worldview. Ask: Why do so many people feel they have to conform to the ways of the world? (answers might include low self-image, need to fit in, need to be accepted, desire to "have fun," and so forth) Ask, What is the difference between teaching information and teaching for transformation? (Teaching for information is little more than lecture-and-leave. Teaching for transformation involves getting personally involved in learners' lives and doing whatever is necessary to help people become more like Christ.) Allow several answers. Then ask: Are you teaching for transformation? If not, what needs to change in your life and teaching?

2 Introduce the importance of a lifestyle that is consistent with the messages we teach. Ask: What kind of leader do you want to follow? List characteristics on a marker board or large sheet of paper. Then use the poster or PowerPoint presentation to overview the five essential traits of effective leaders in chapter 2 (5-7 minutes). Ask: What could happen in a group whose leader lacks one of these traits? For example, what kind of group would you have if your teacher lacked character? Vision? A servant heart? Present a minilecture on the section "The Price of Leadership" (3-5 minutes). Call attention to the need for teachers who live and serve as Jesus did. Close this activity with a strong emphasis on how the leader is the lesson, and must be conscious of the role of leader before learners and others at all times.

3 Form groups by generational group, breaking the groups out based on one of the generational structures recommended in chapter 3. Choose the one that most nearly matches the organizational structure used in your Bible study group ministry. Ask each group to review the implications listed in the chapter for each age group. Assign each group the following: Based on the implications for ministry with the age group you are assigned, make a list of actions that could be taken to address each of the implications. (Allow 5 minutes.) Have each group present a one-minute overview of actions they would recommend. Allow other participants to add ideas to the lists. Record these ideas and then provide the suggestions later to all participants.

4 Ask, Why can following a guide be important sometimes? Who should be our guide day by day? (Jesus, through the Bible) Present the poster displaying the seven principles identified in chapter 5. Give a one-minute review of each principle. Distribute plain sheets of paper to everyone. Ask participants to reflect on the importance they place on each of these principles, and then ask them to write a statement of what they feel they need to do to strengthen these principles in their lives. Ask workers to form accountability groups of three or four and to develop a list of ways to work together to encourage accountability. Remind workers this is not intended to embarrass anyone, but to help workers become more effective as transformational teachers. If someone chooses not to participate, affirm that person and encourage that person to develop a way to improve independently.

5 Ask: Is your Bible study group open or closed? What makes you think this to be true? What is the purpose of your Bible study group? Allow time for several answers. Comment on the nature and purpose of Bible study groups based on "Understanding the Group's Purpose and Nature" in chapter 6. Then present a minilecture of open and closed Bible study groups (3-5 minutes). Emphasize the importance of open groups as the foundation for Bible study through the Sunday School. Ask participants to suggest ways to assure that your Sunday School group remains an open group.

Remind workers that open groups are to be intentionally evangelistic. Ask: How important is it to reach the lost? After several answers, ask: How many lost people have come to faith in Christ through your Bible study group in the last year? Why haven't more people come to Christ through your group? What hinders your group from being an evangelistic Bible study group? Explain why some Bible study groups must be evangelism centers based on the content of chapter 7. Ask: When was the last time your group enrolled an unsaved person? Why does a group stop reaching lost people? (no commitment to evangelism, no burden for the lost, no desire from members to move outside their comfort zones) What must we do to make our Bible study groups truly evangelistic?

6 Begin by defining *ministry environment* based on chapter 12. Point out that the ministry environment is much more than just the facilities, including: equipment, relationships, group mission, vision, lesson preparation and presentation, organizational structure, attitudes of leaders, and so forth. Ask: When is most effort invested in creating a positive ministry environment? (before the session) Emphasize that teachers must **prepare** a strong ministry environment. Note that regular leadership meetings are important to creating a positive ministry environment. Lead participants to brainstorm activities that could be included in weekly leadership meetings, based on chapter 8. (3-5 minutes) Present ideas from chapter 12 that can enhance preparation efforts, lesson application, and fellowship. Point out that being a good teacher means developing skills beyond the classroom, such as being a good listener. These skills contribute to a good ministry environment. If you have the Leader Training Pack, use the Kit Item 7, "Developing Listening Skills" Listening Sheet to present a minilecture on how to be a good listener. A PowerPoint presentation for this and additional background information are provided on the CD-ROM.

7 Ask, what makes a Bible study effective? Point out that leading adults to spiritual transformation requires good preparation and presentation. Transformation requires a personal **encounter** with the living, life-changing Word of God. Leaders can prepare for life-changing Bible study encounters. Present a minilecture on the section "The Seven Elements of Transformational Learning" from chapter 9 (7-10 minutes). Give careful attention to each of the elements, and point out that the words in bold letters sum up each of the statements (for example, context is a word that summarizes the section Personalize